The Art of Icky Dog

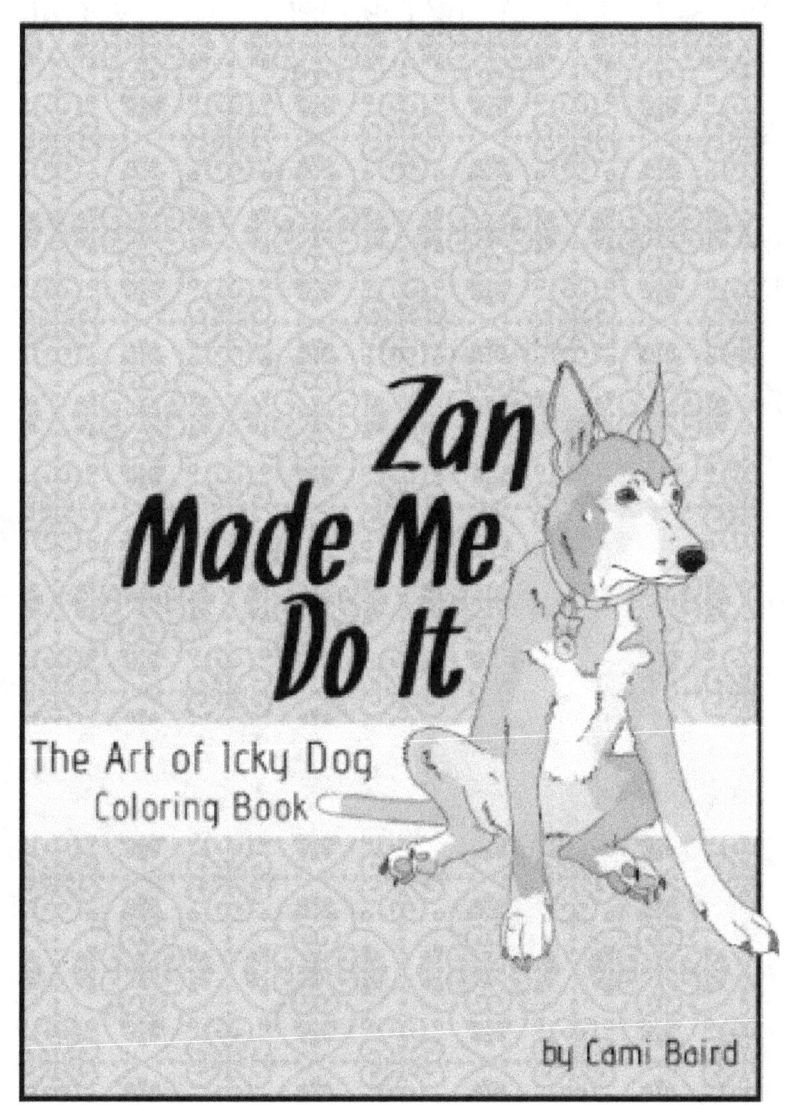

Zan Made Me Do It

The Art of Icky Dog
Coloring Book

by Cami Baird

Printed in the United States of America
First Printing, 2018
Printed by CreateSpace, An Amazon.com Company
ISBN 13:978-198208129
ISBN 10:1982080124

Icky Dog Creations
Bairje@Hotmail.com
https://ickydog.deviantart.com/

Cut this page out, and place it behind the page you are coloring. This will help elemenate the marker color bleeding through to the next coloring page.

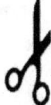

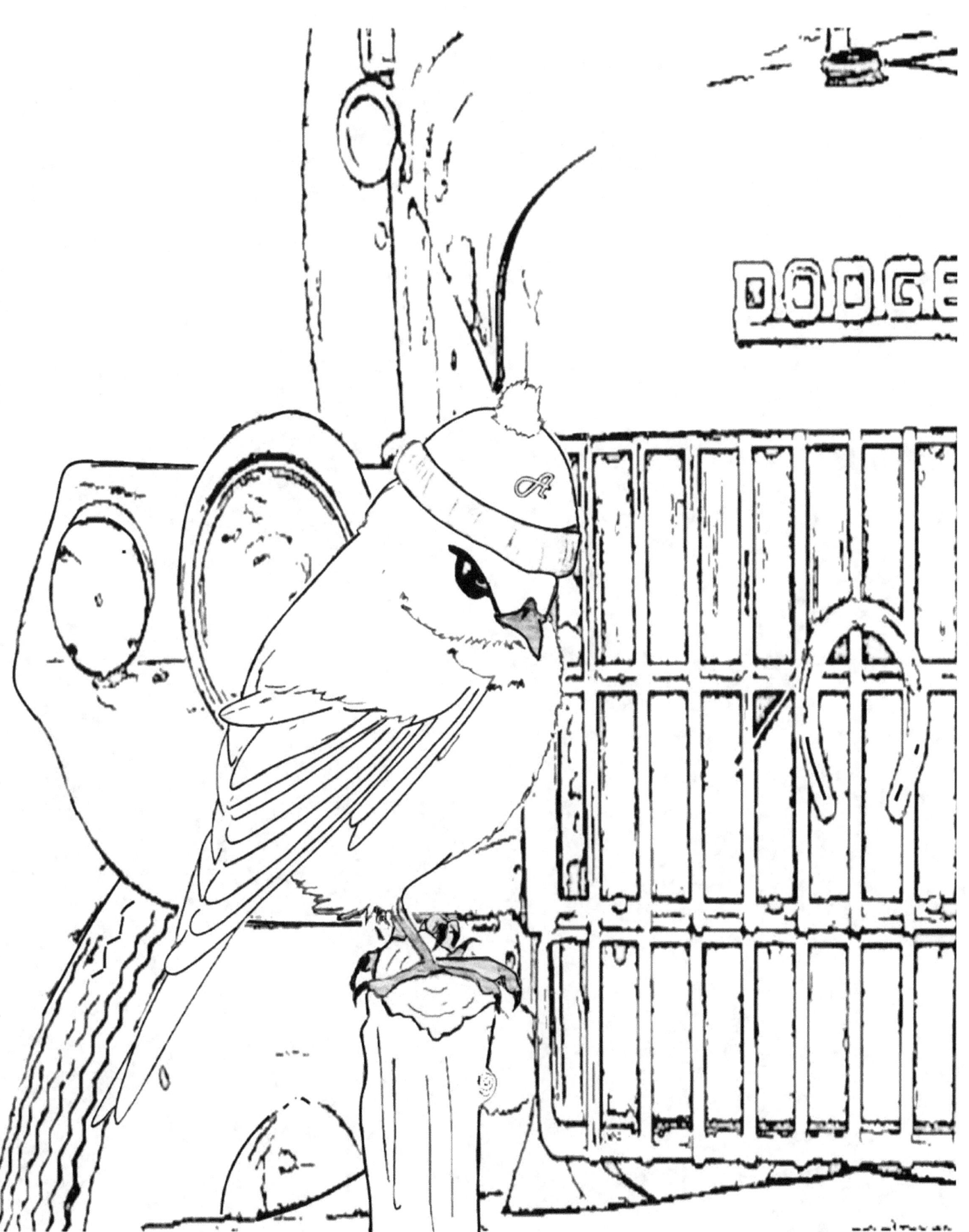

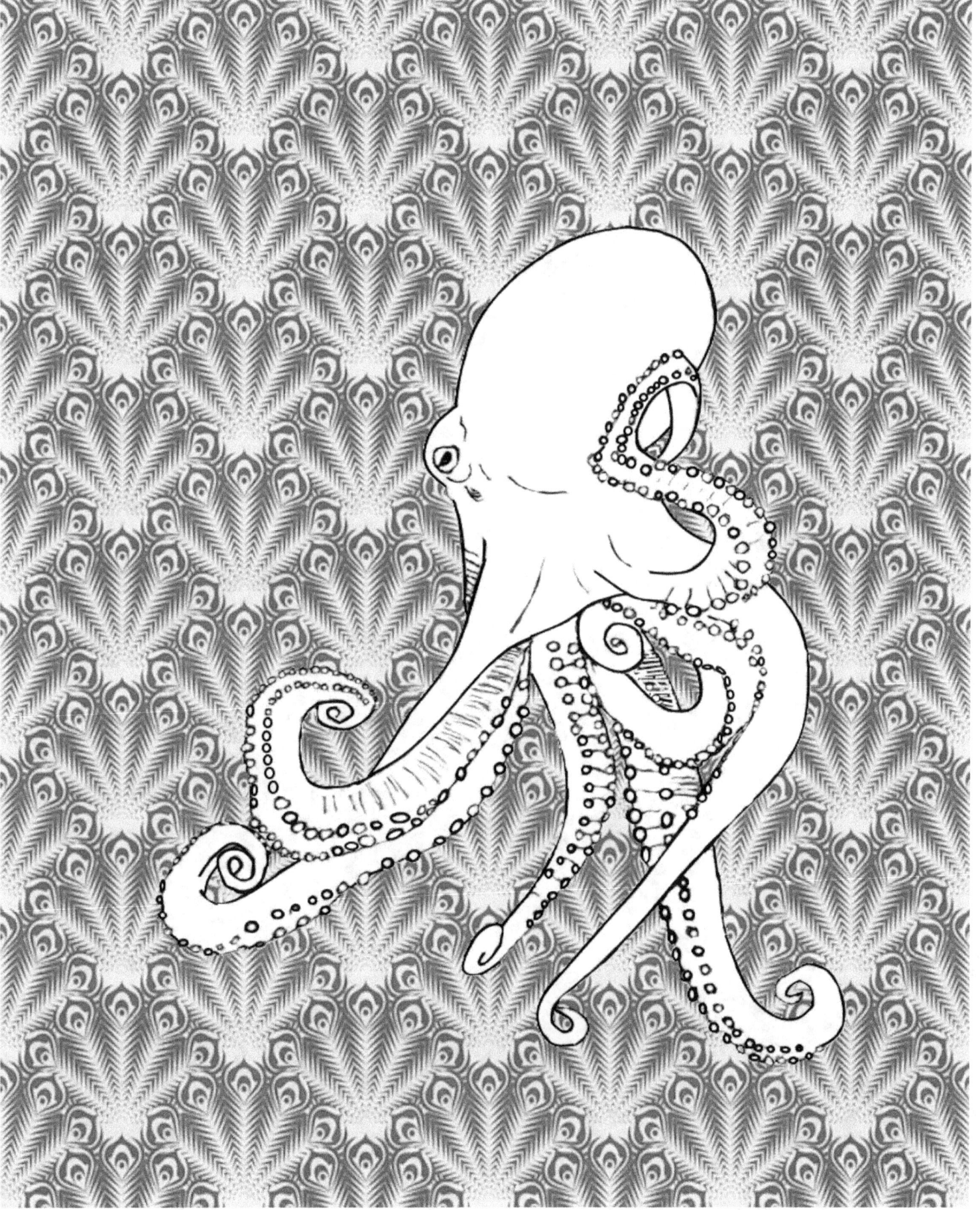

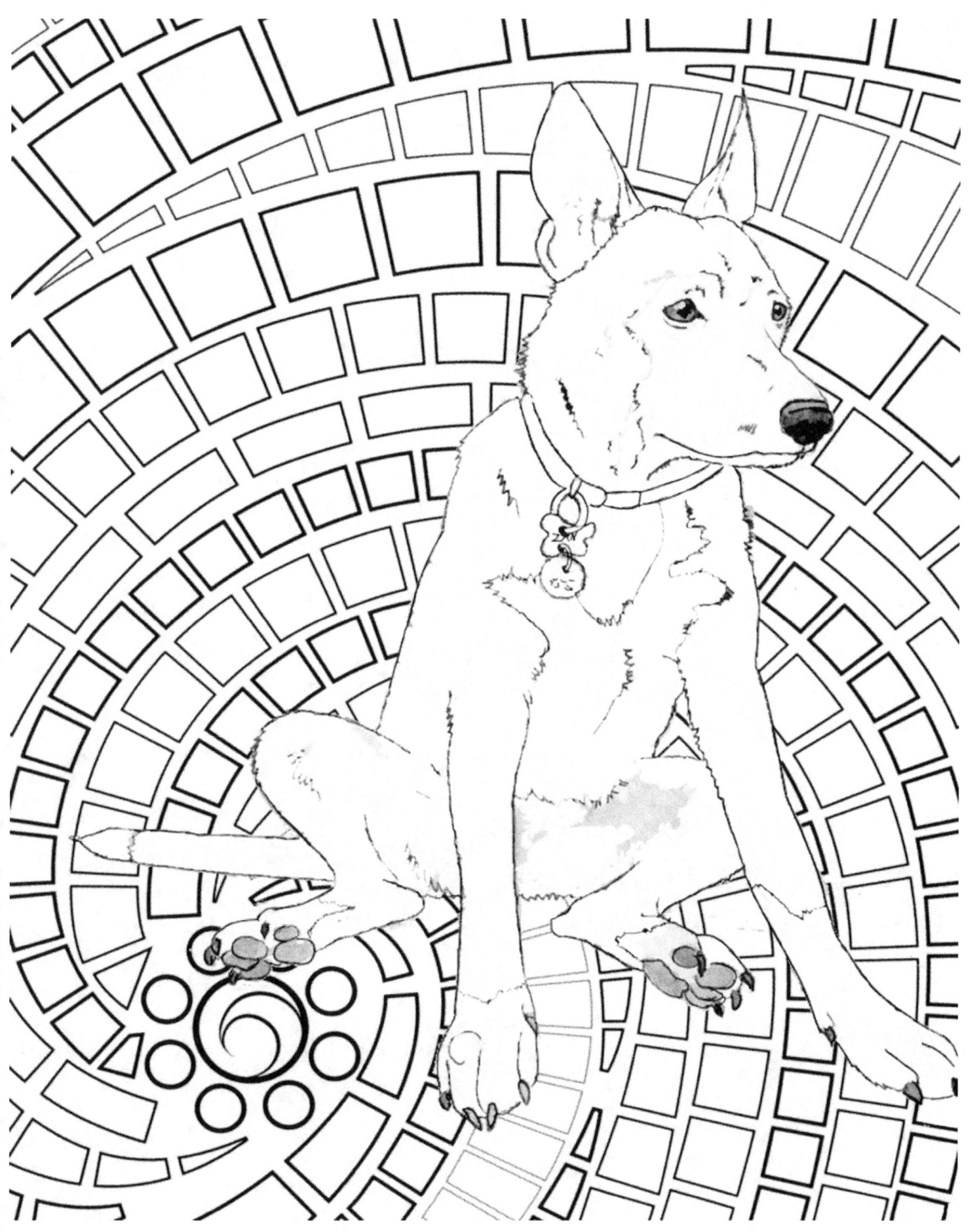

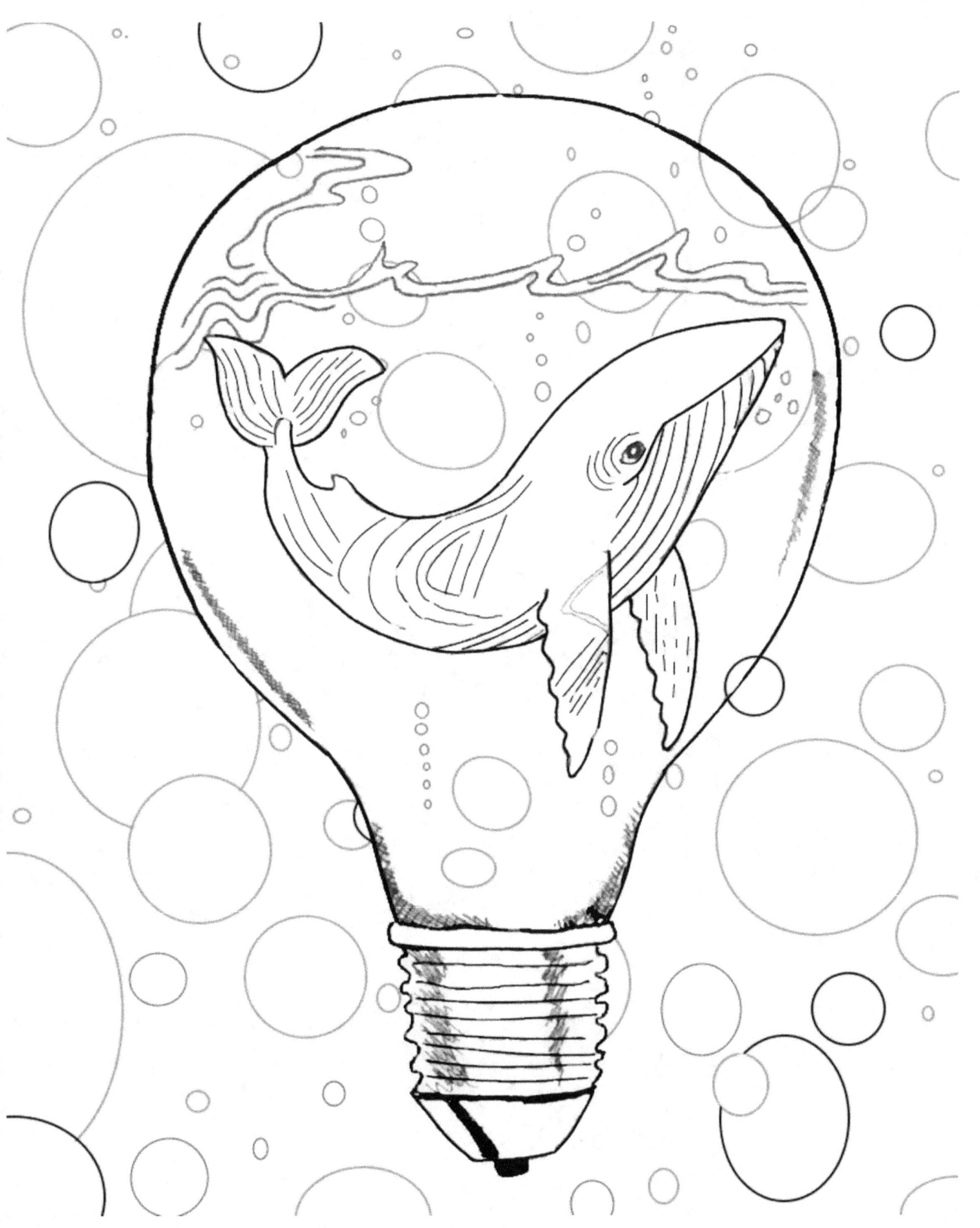

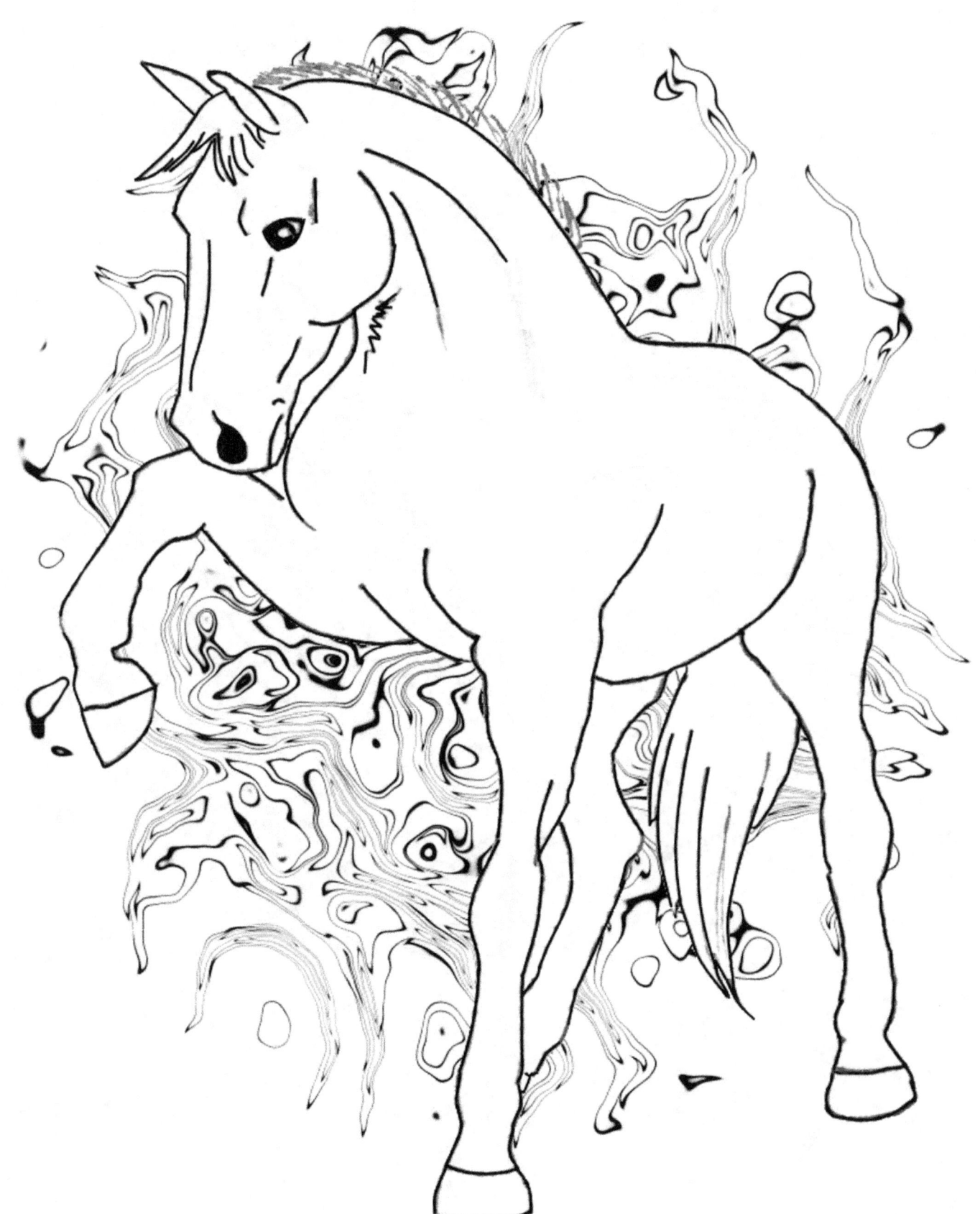

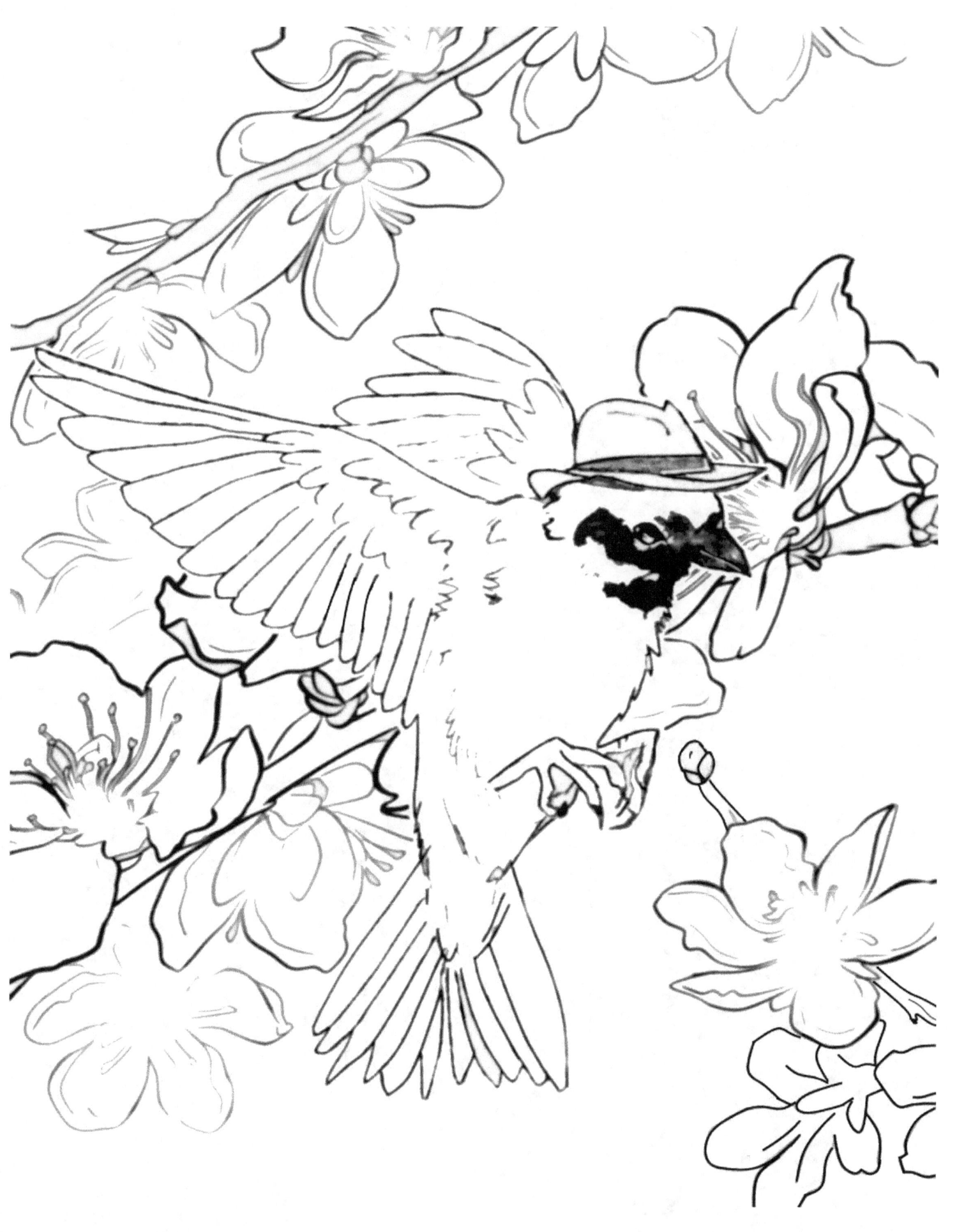

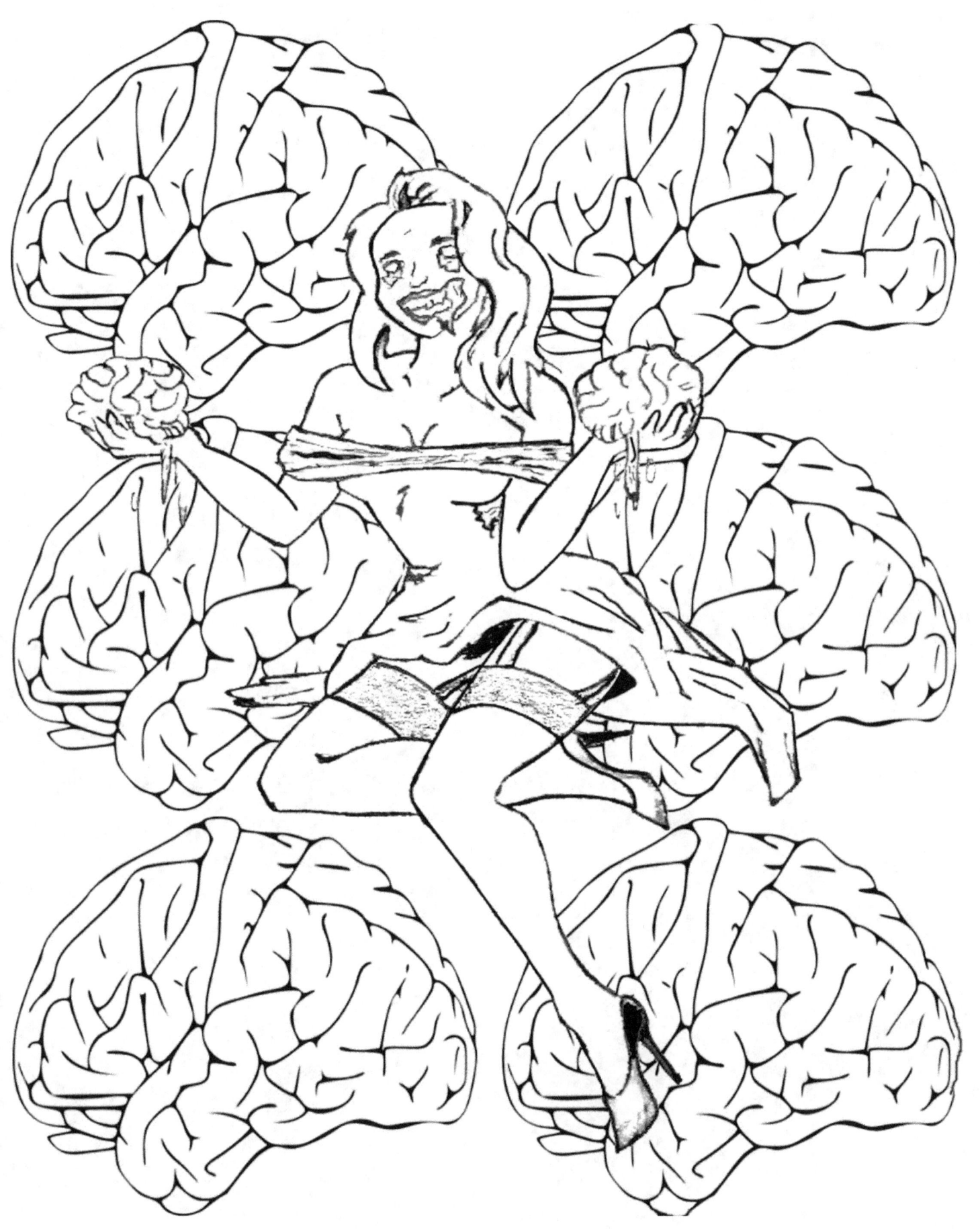

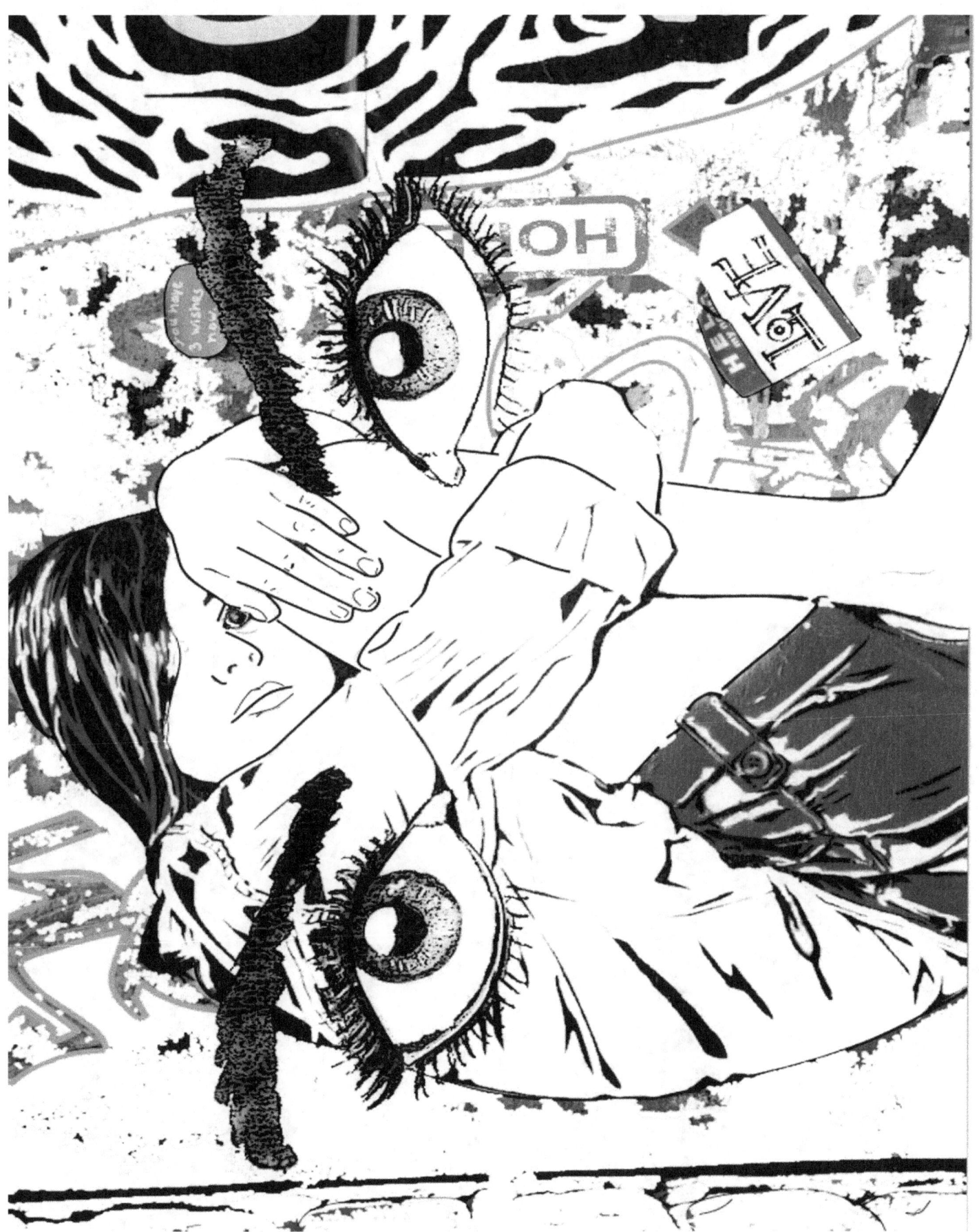

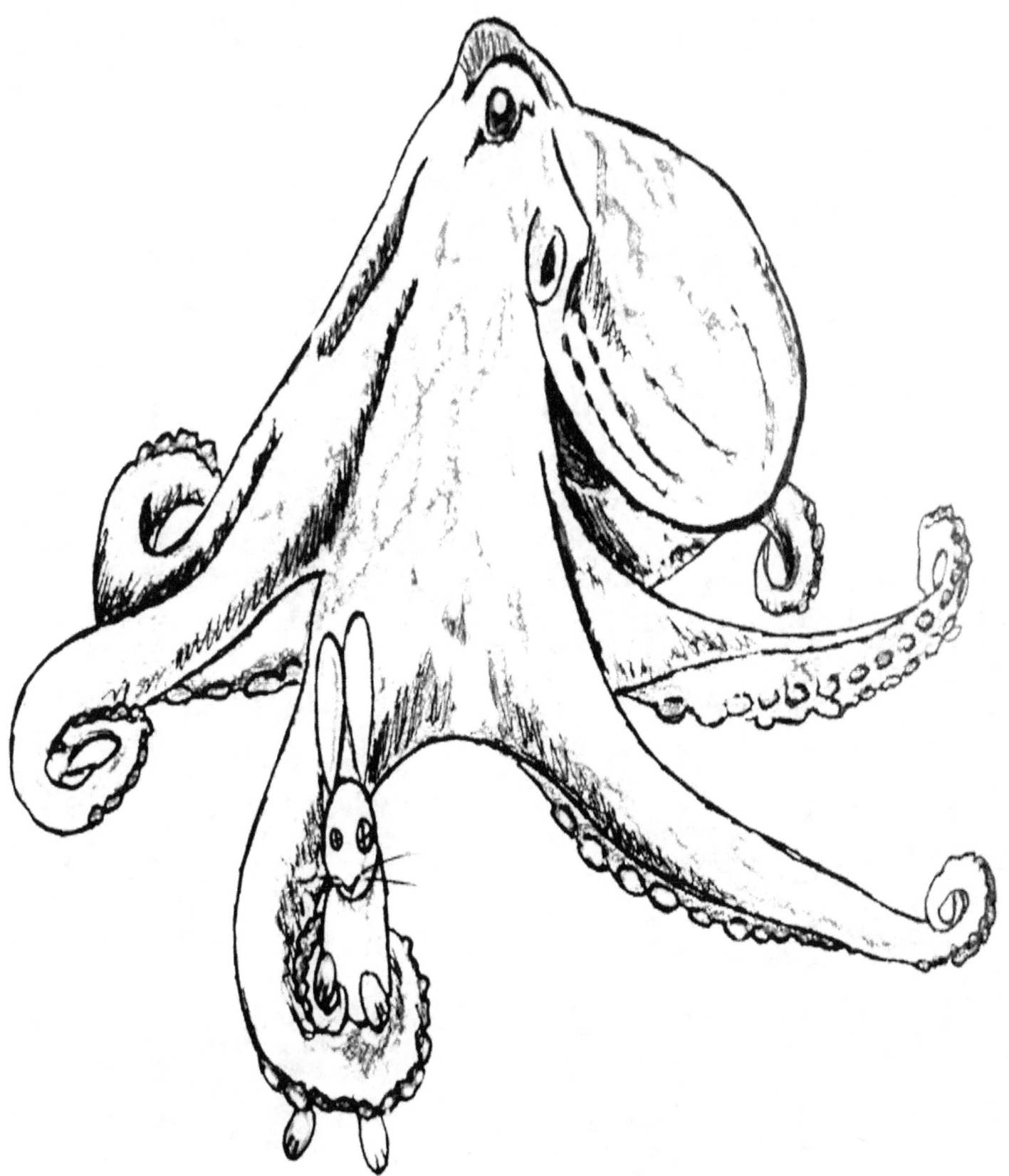

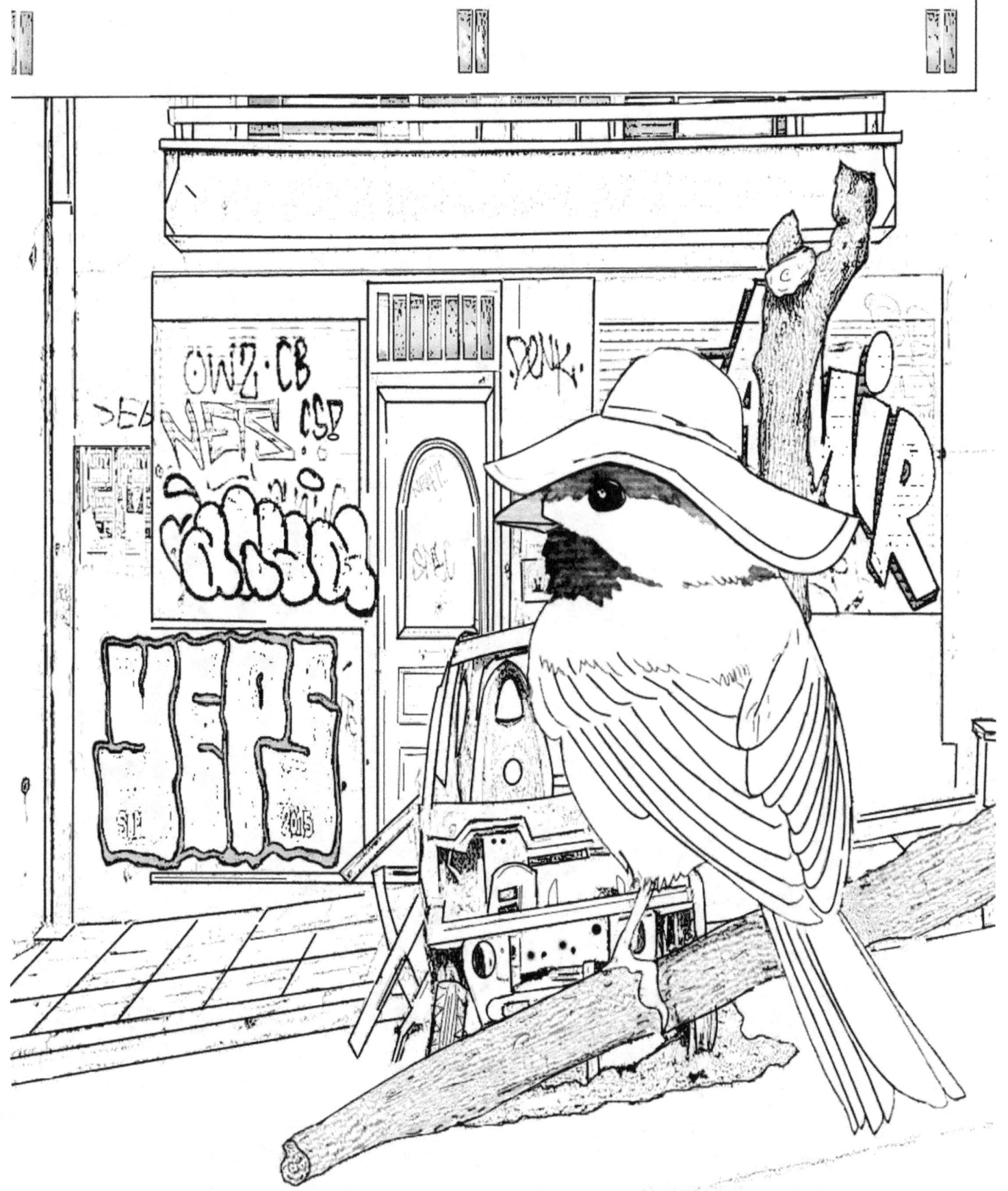

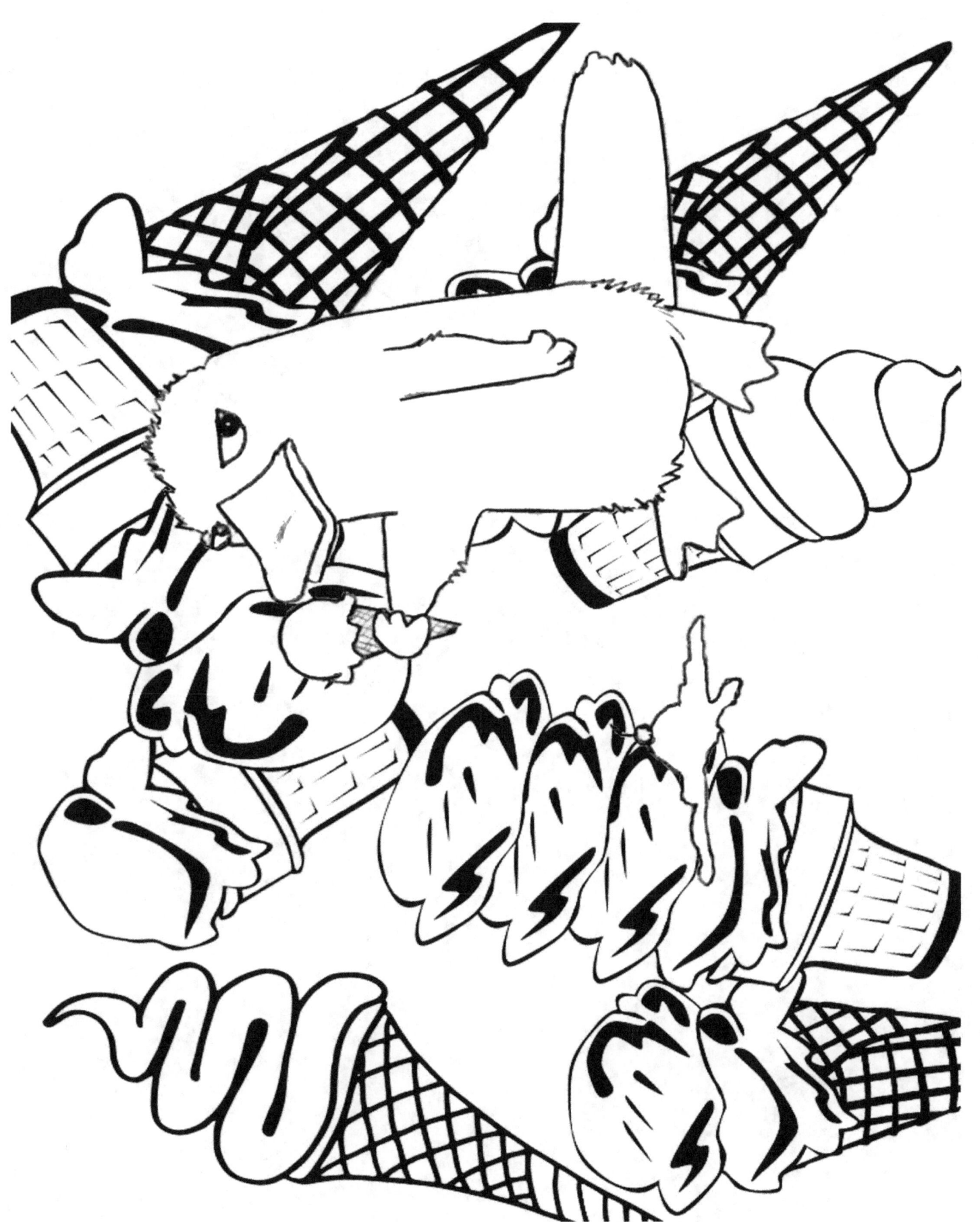

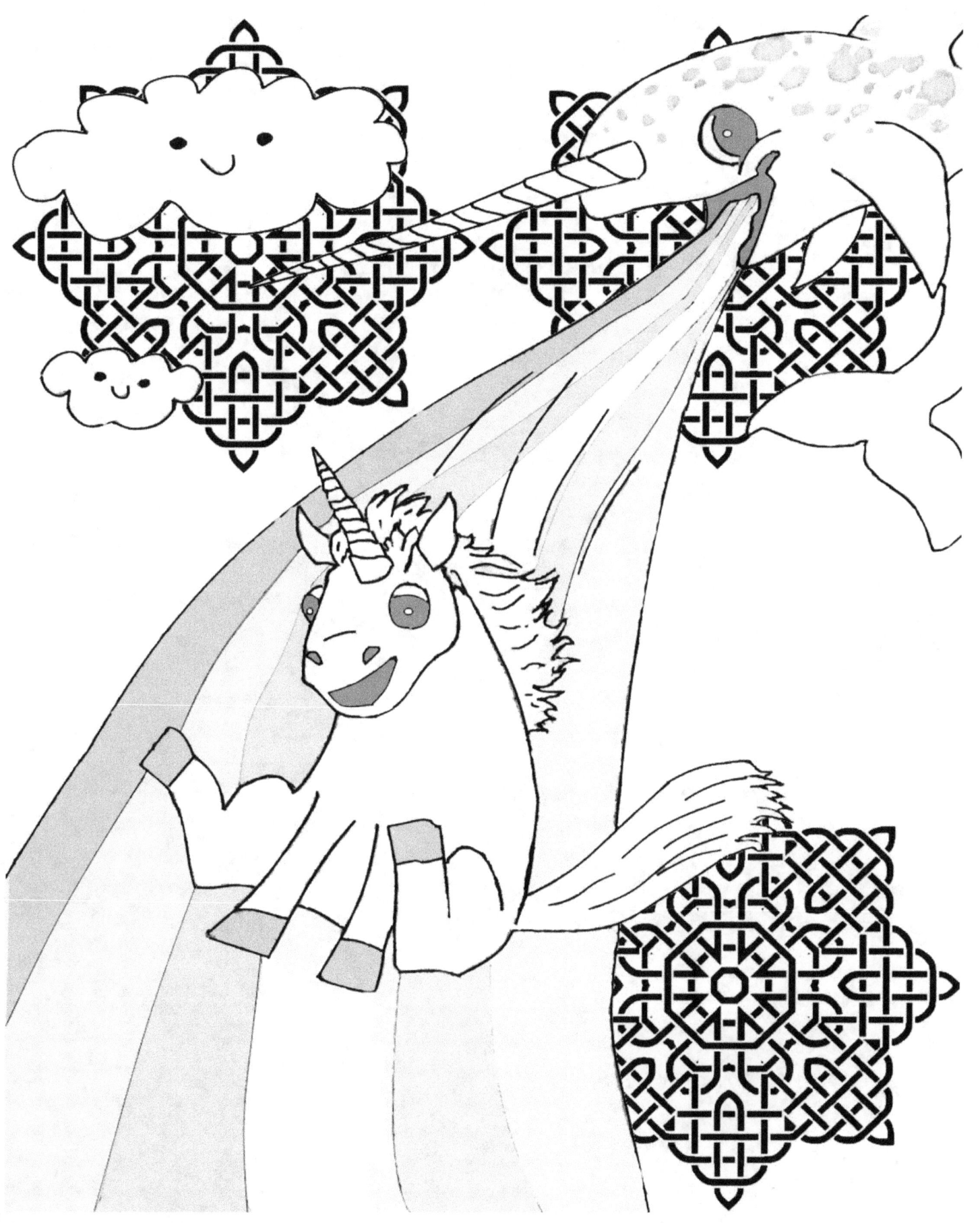

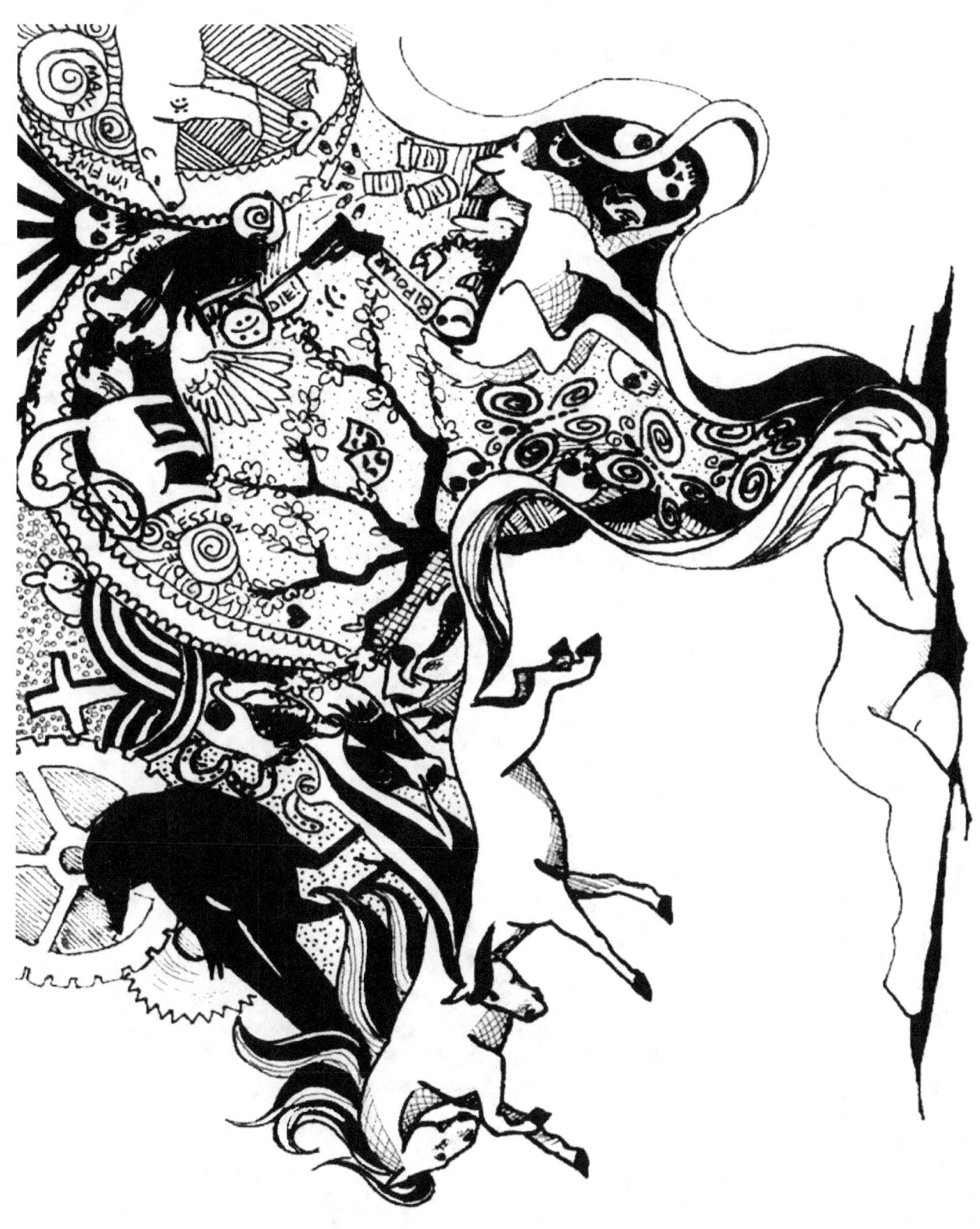

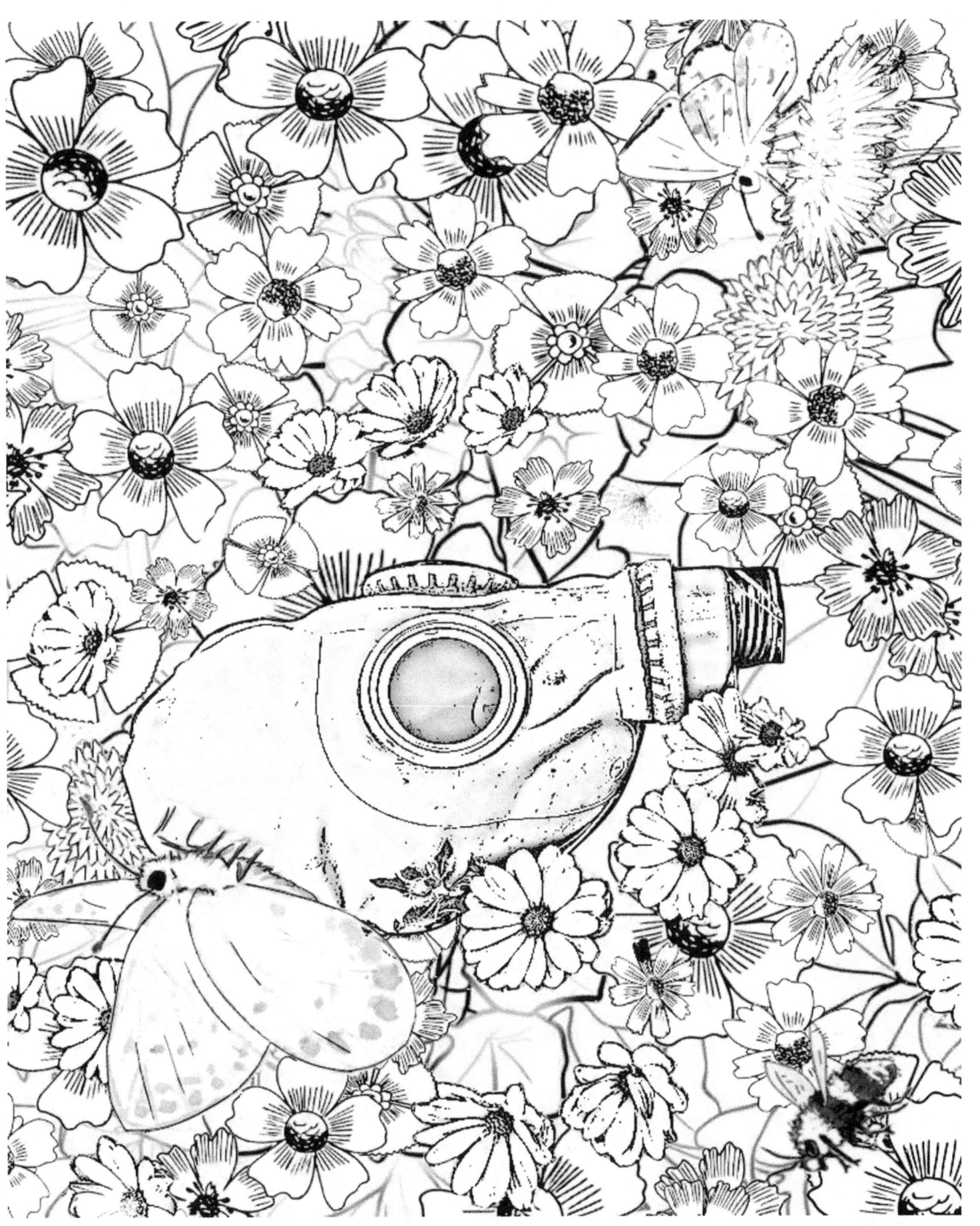

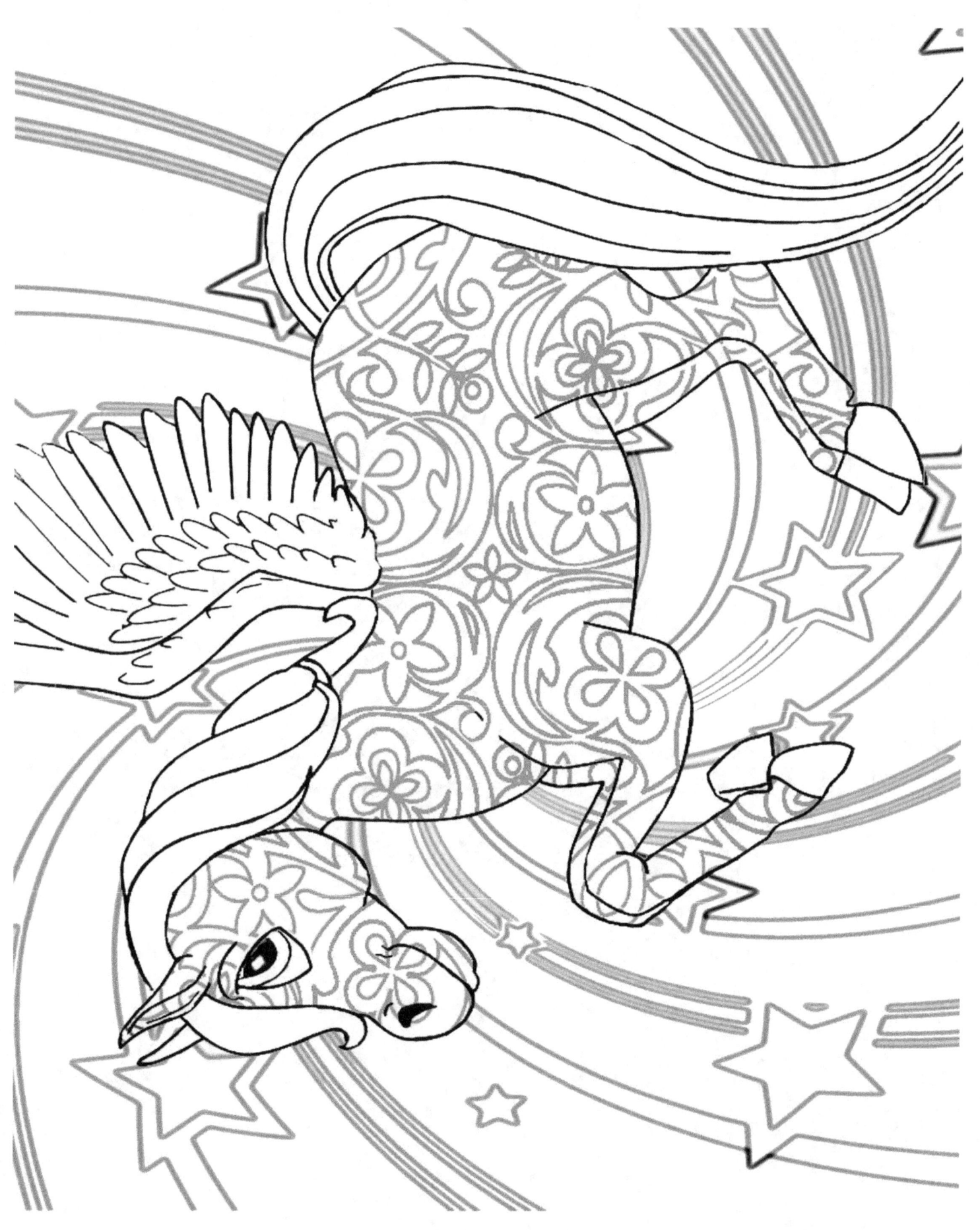

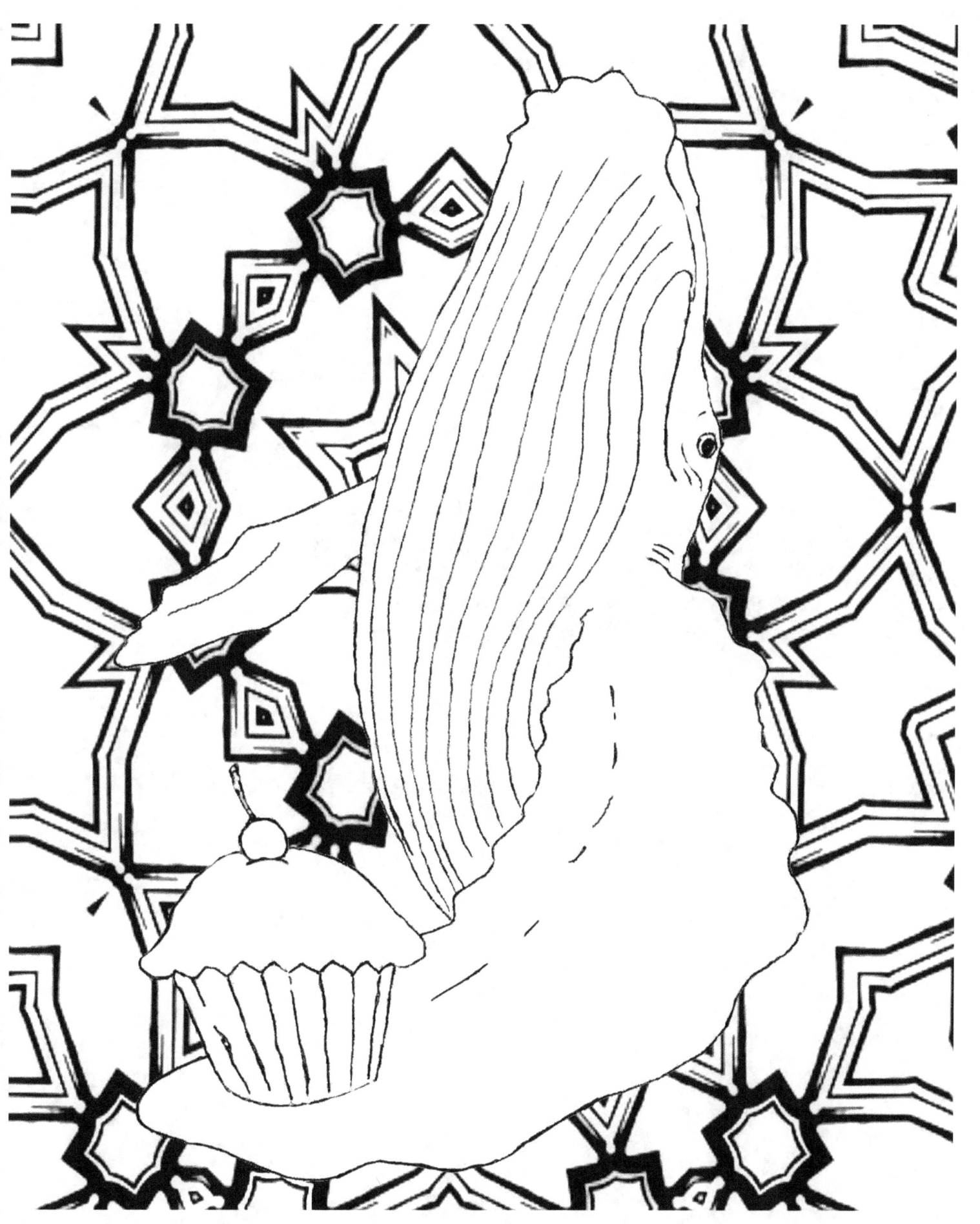

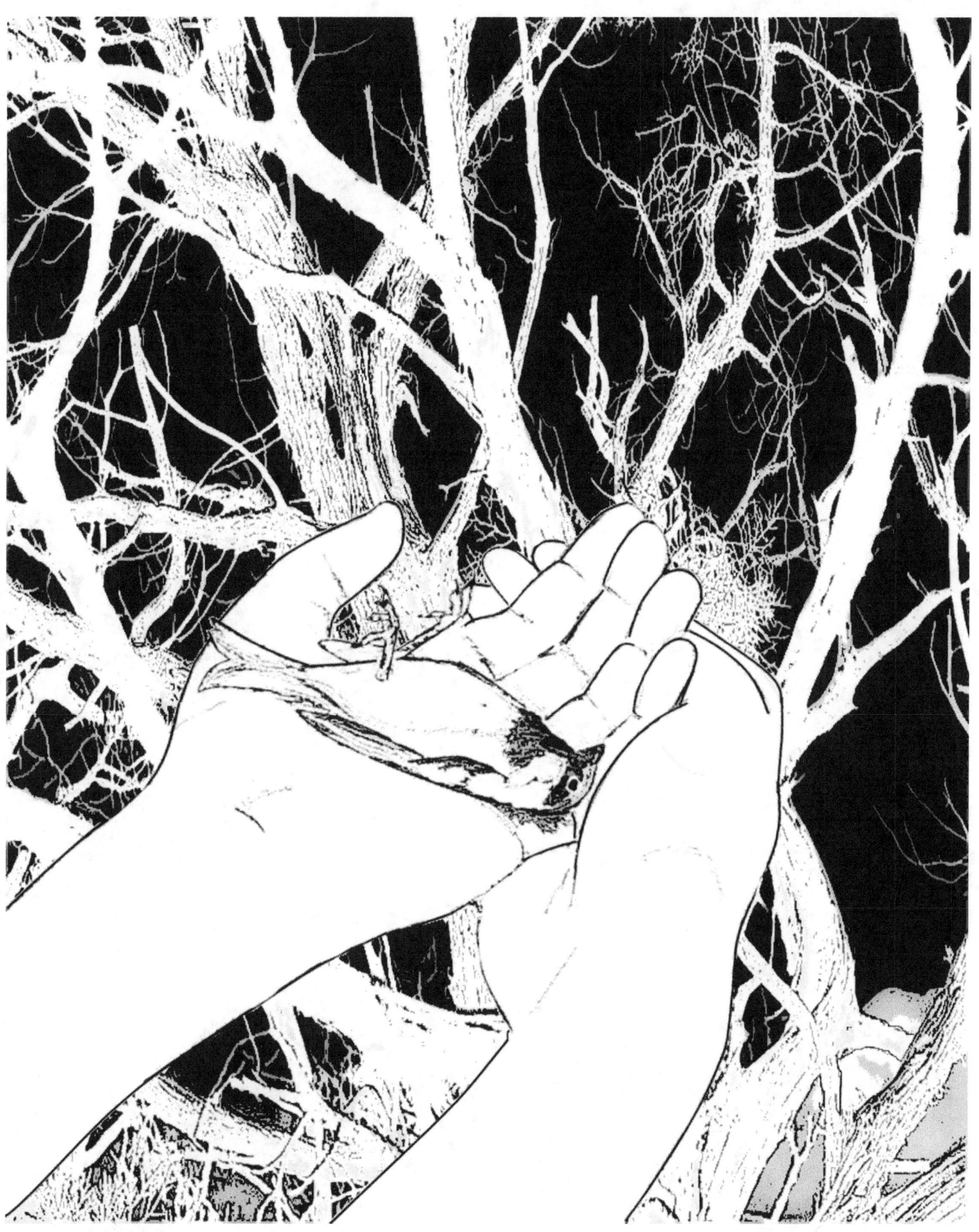

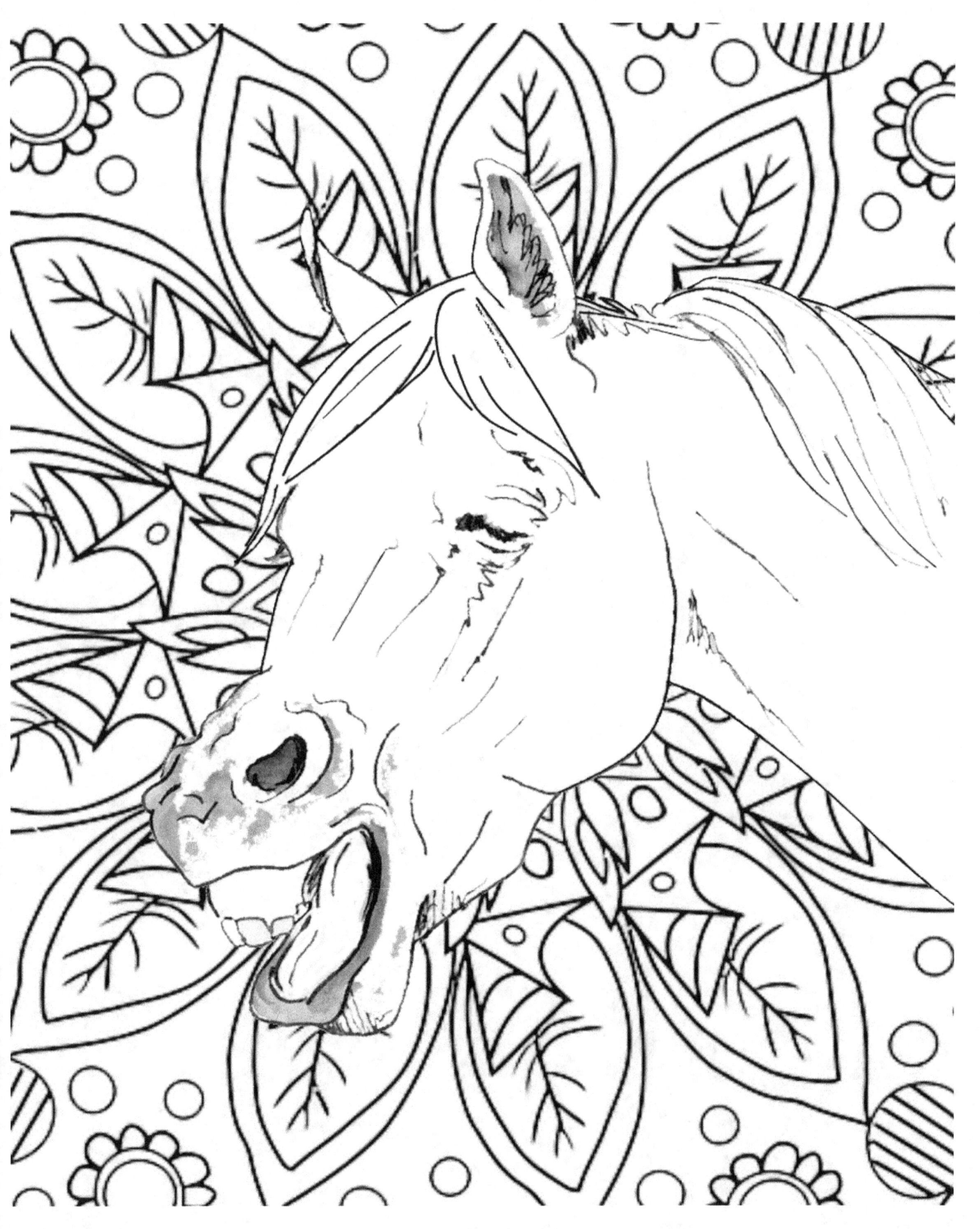

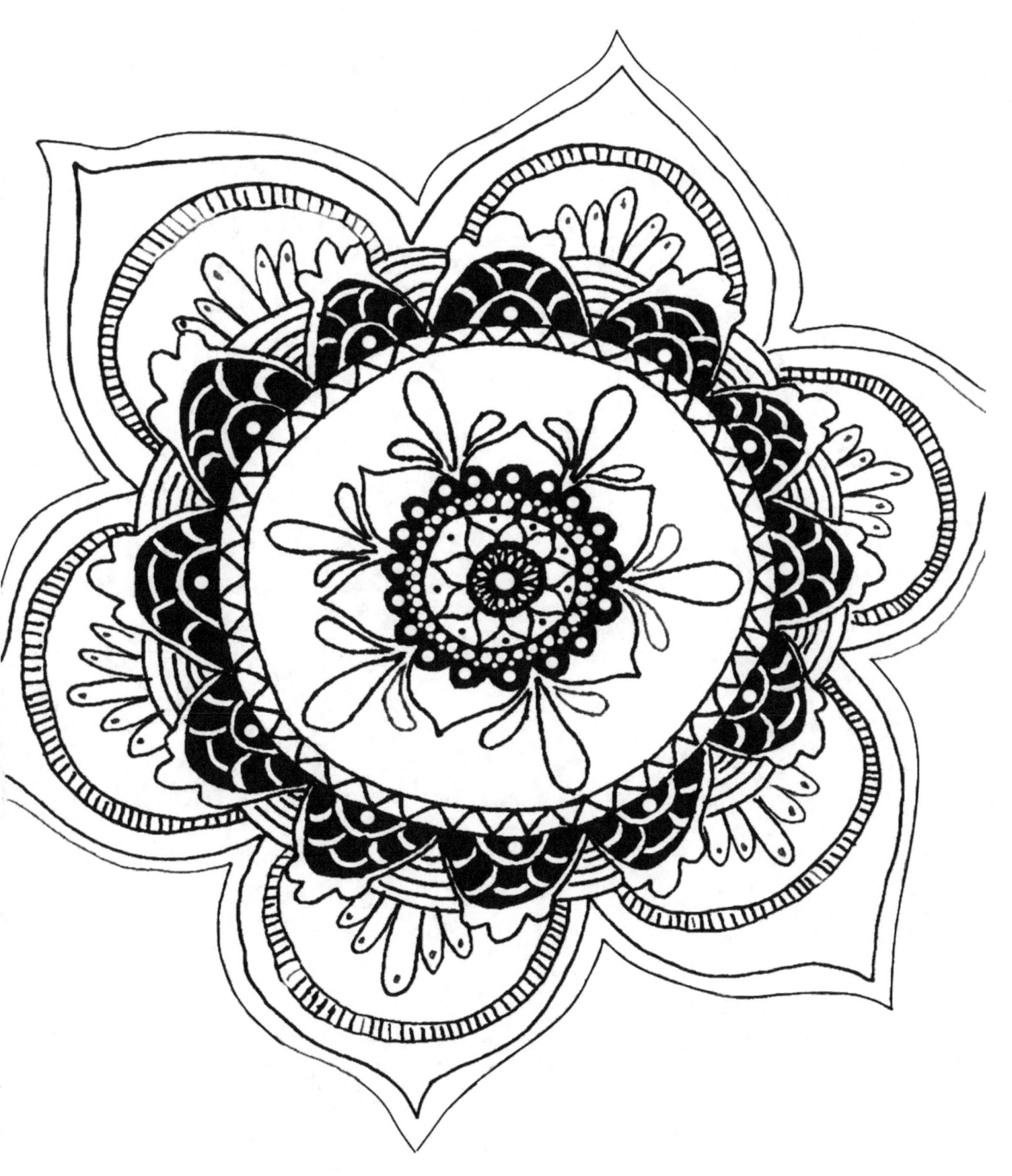

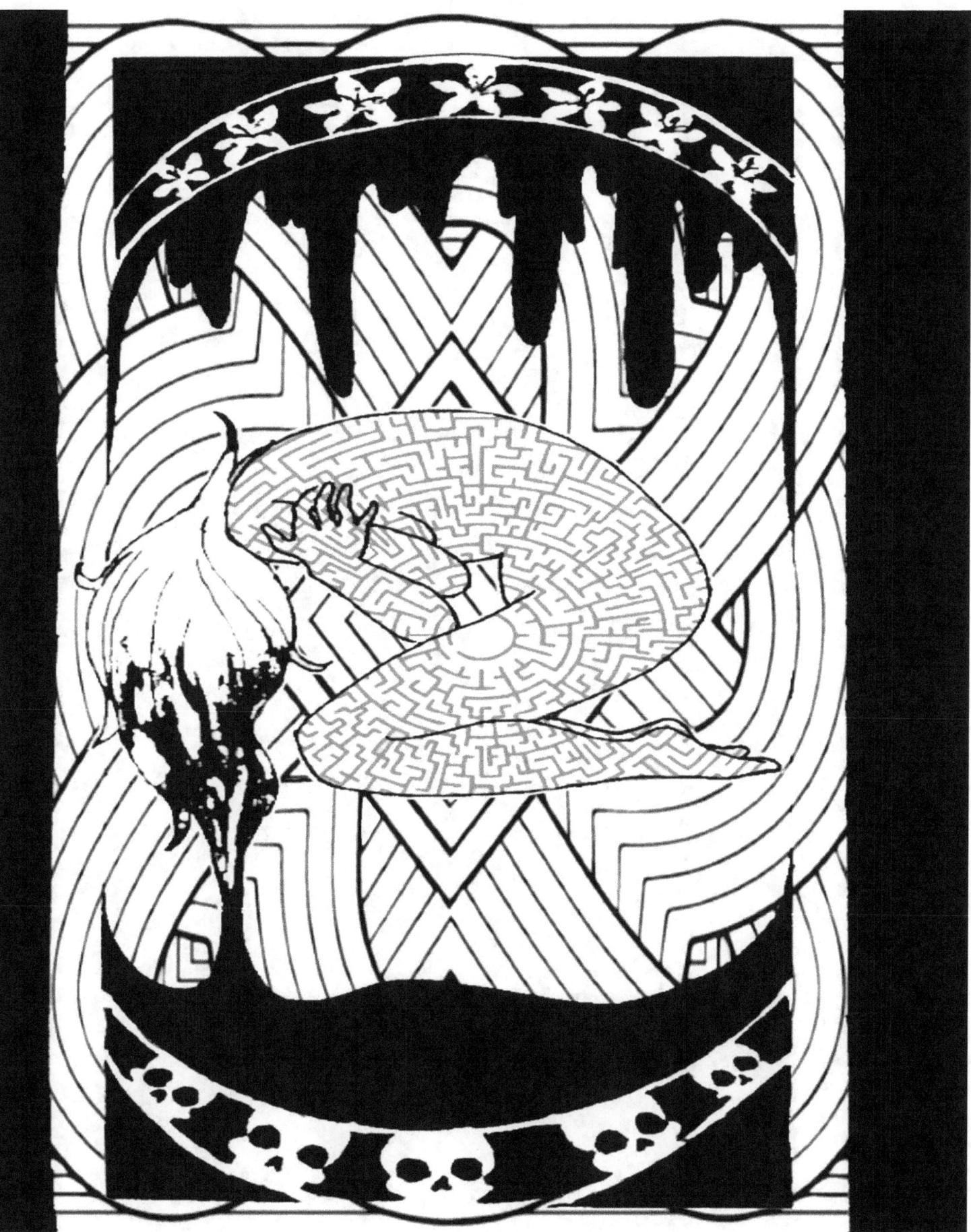

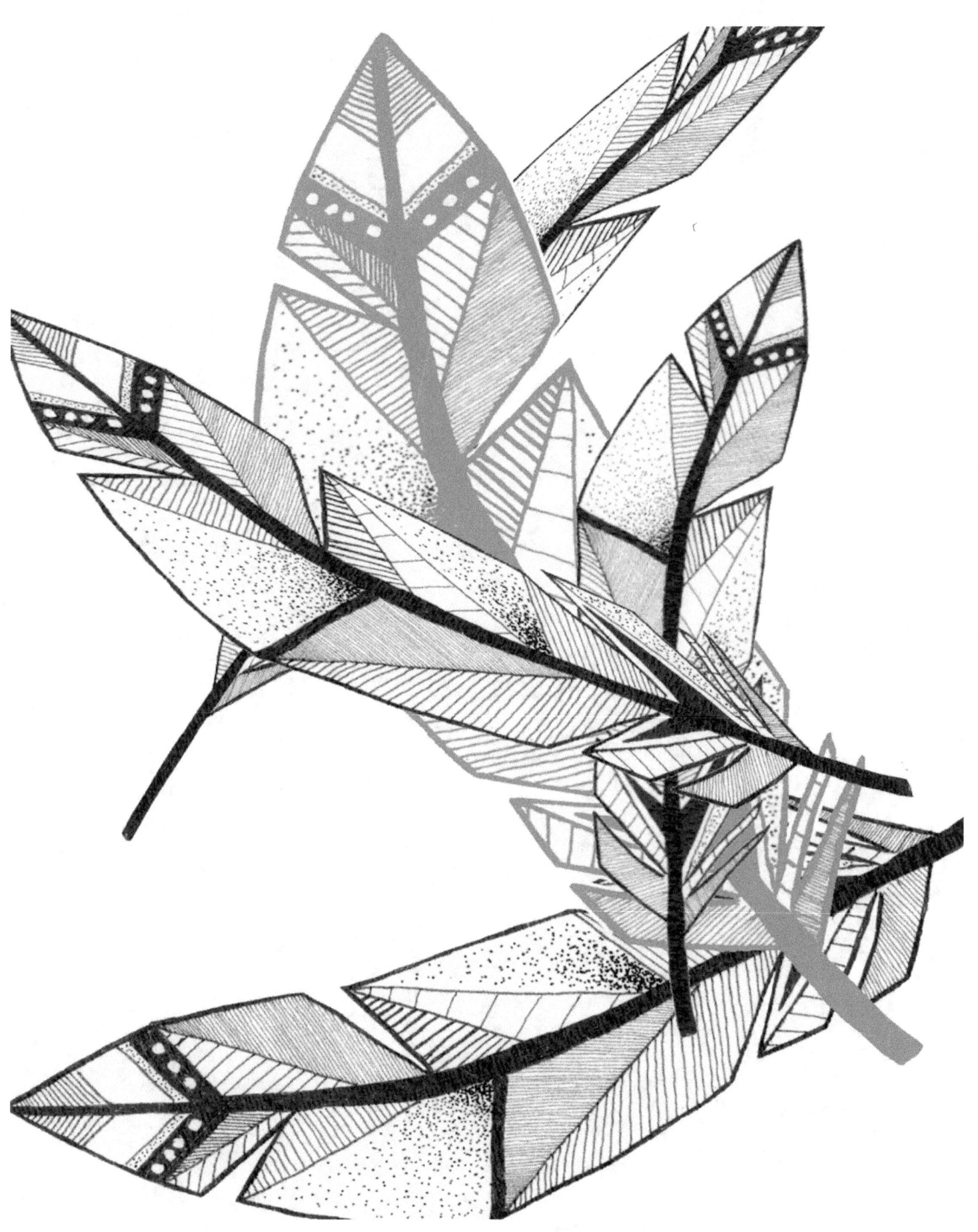

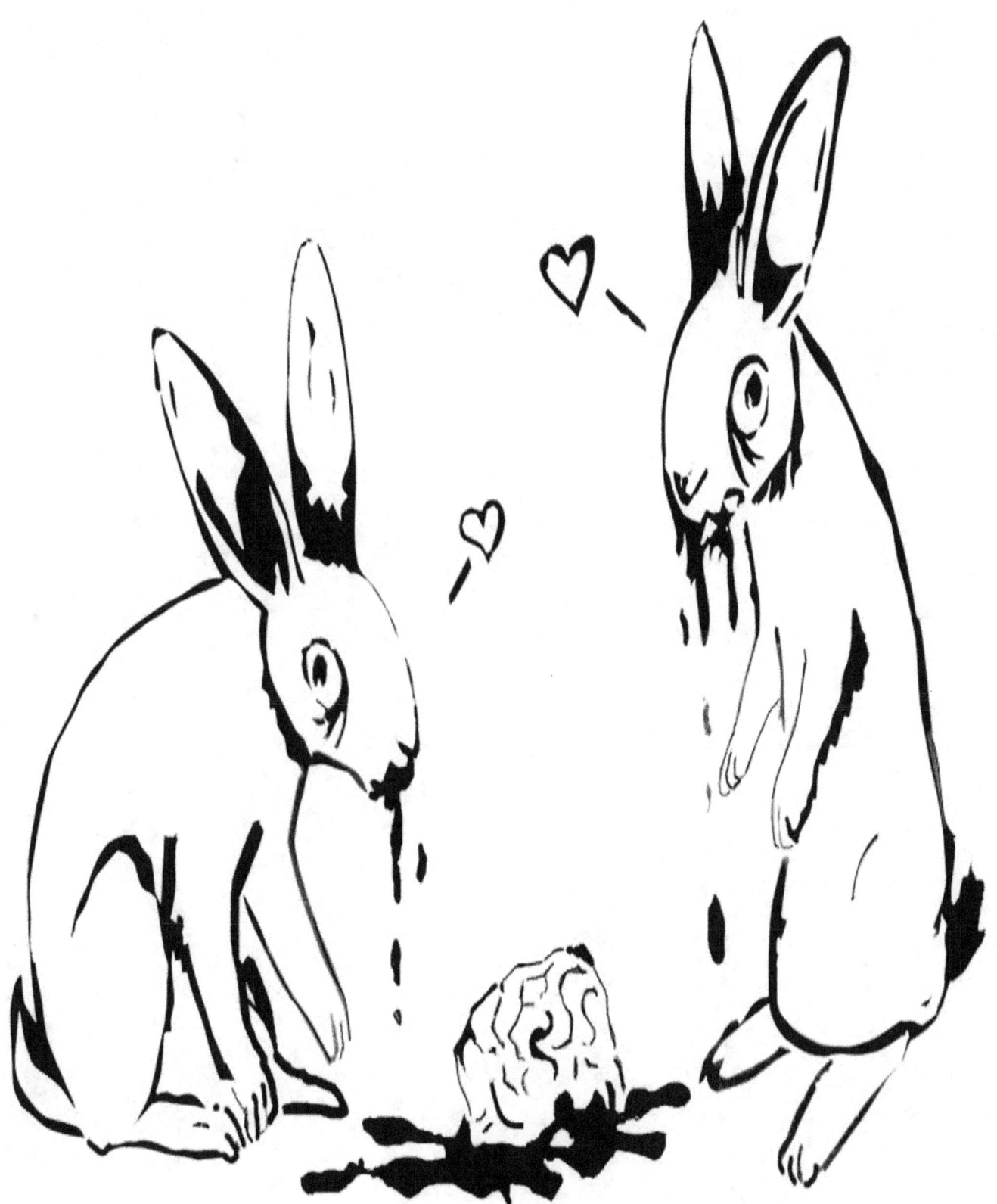

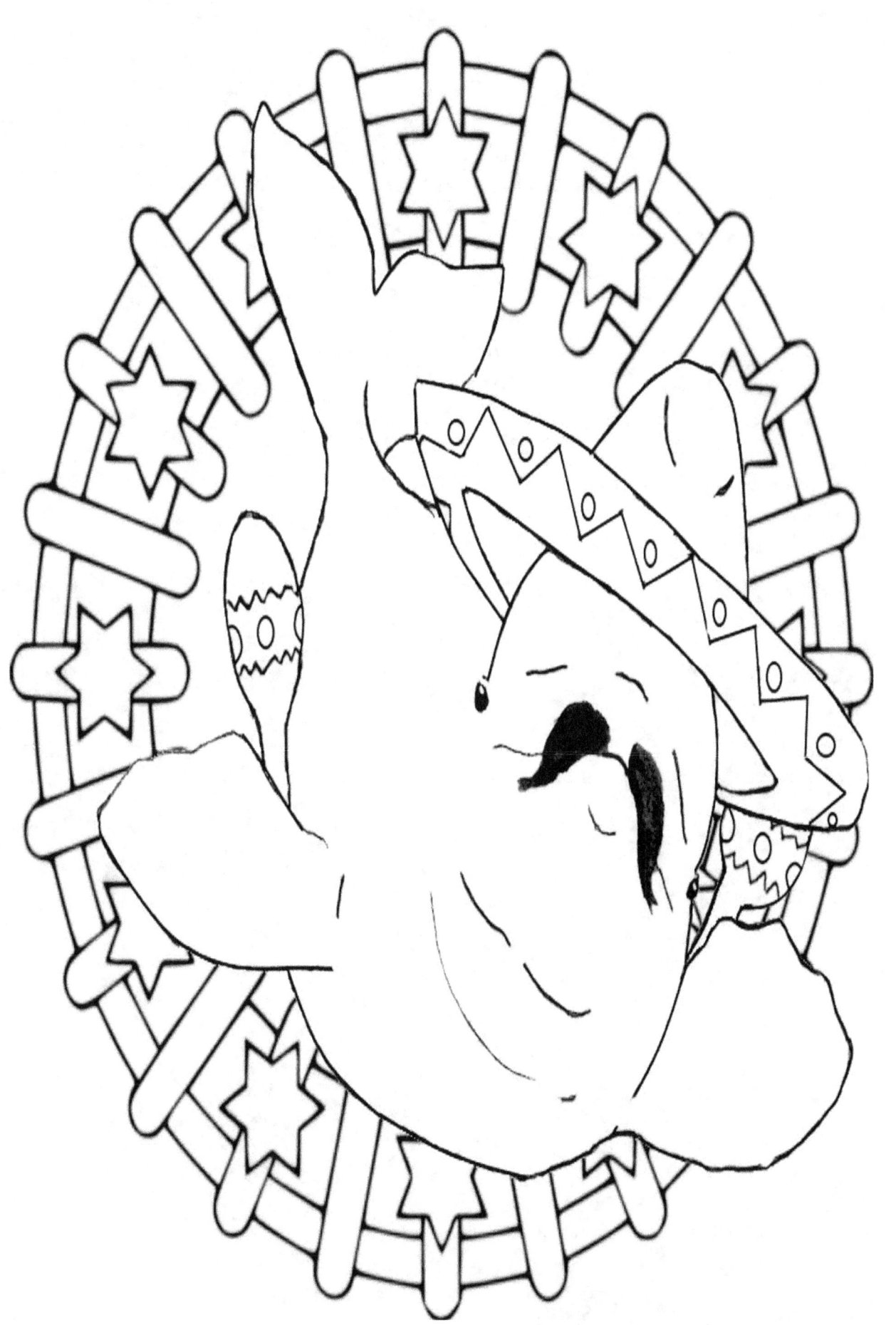

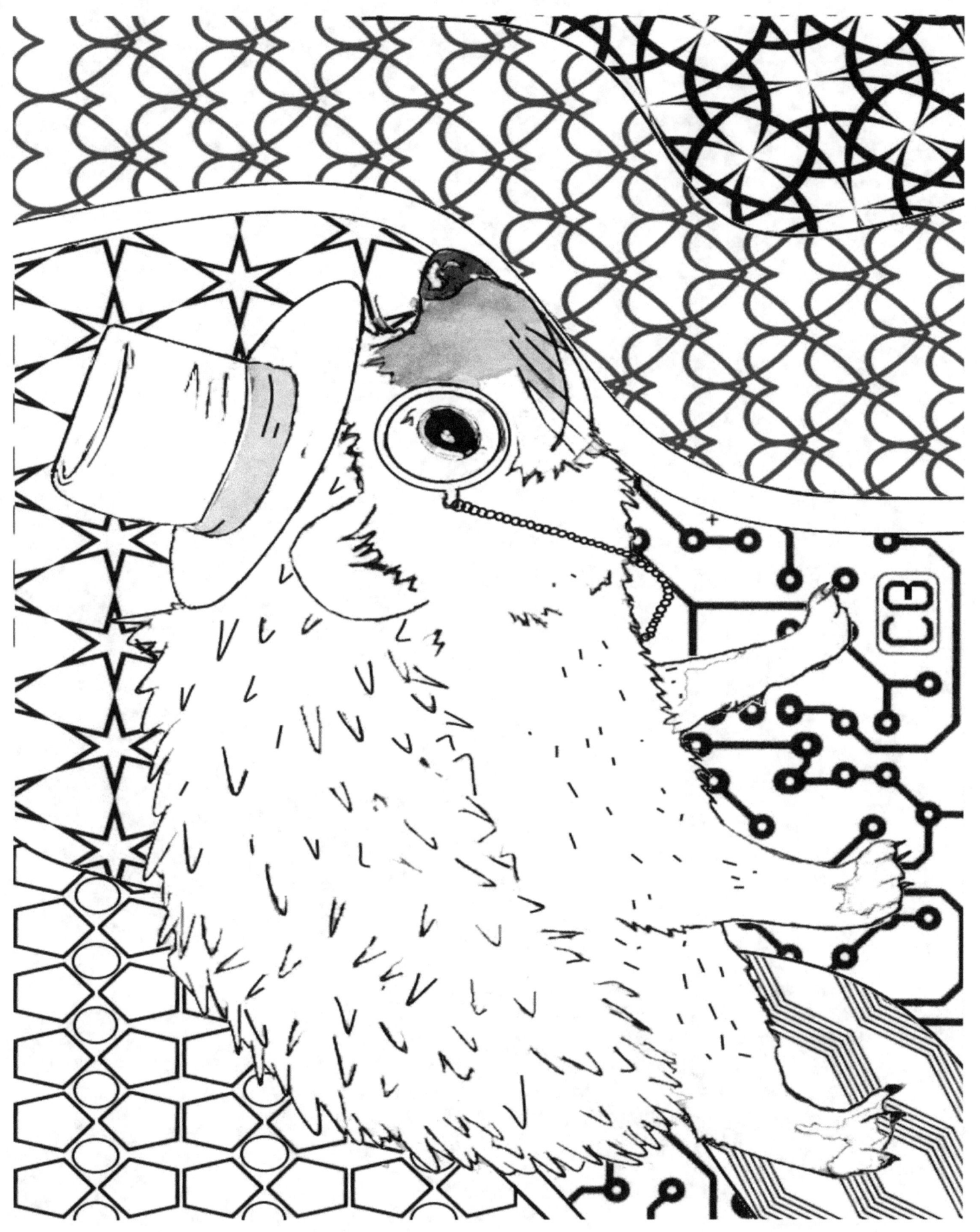

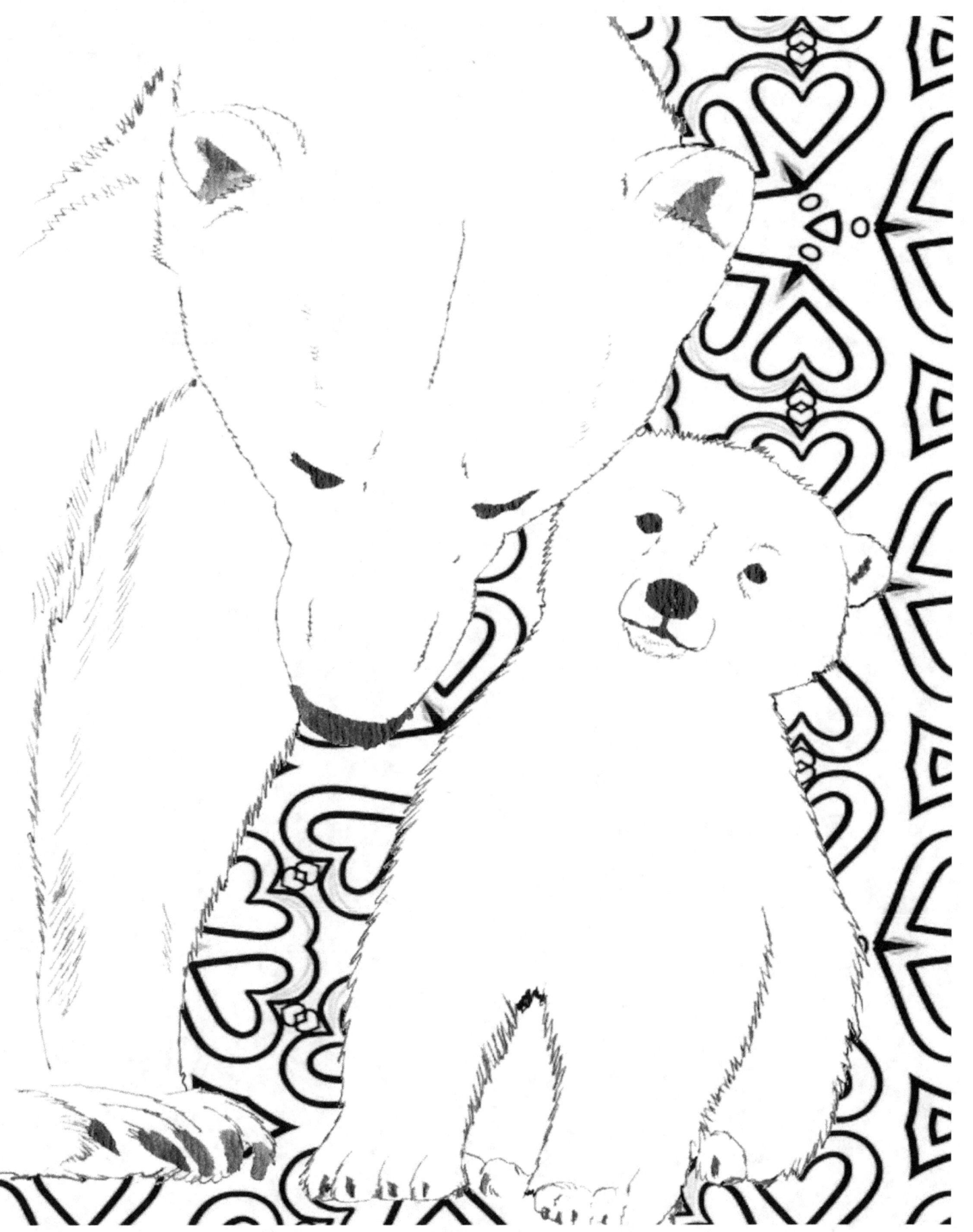

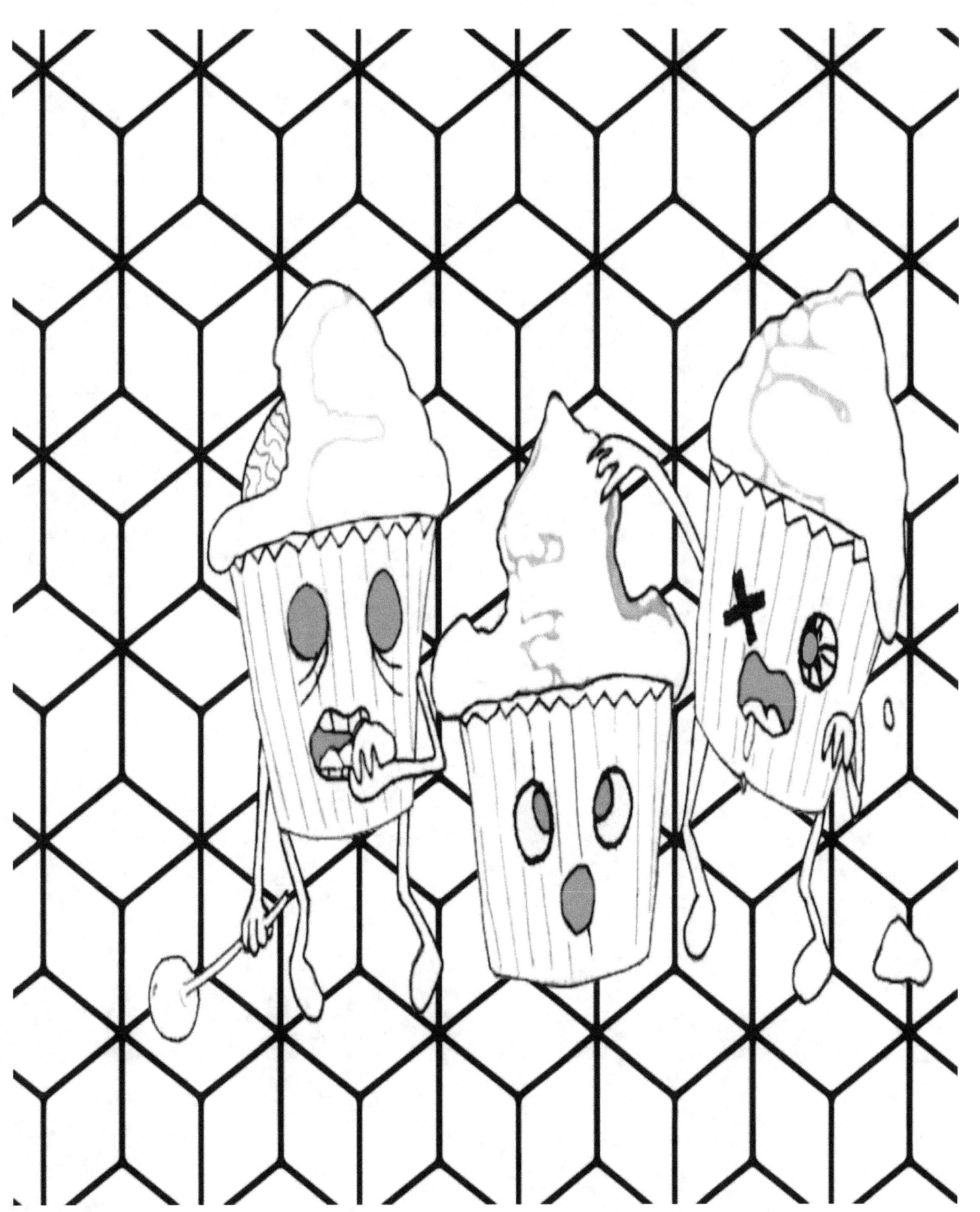

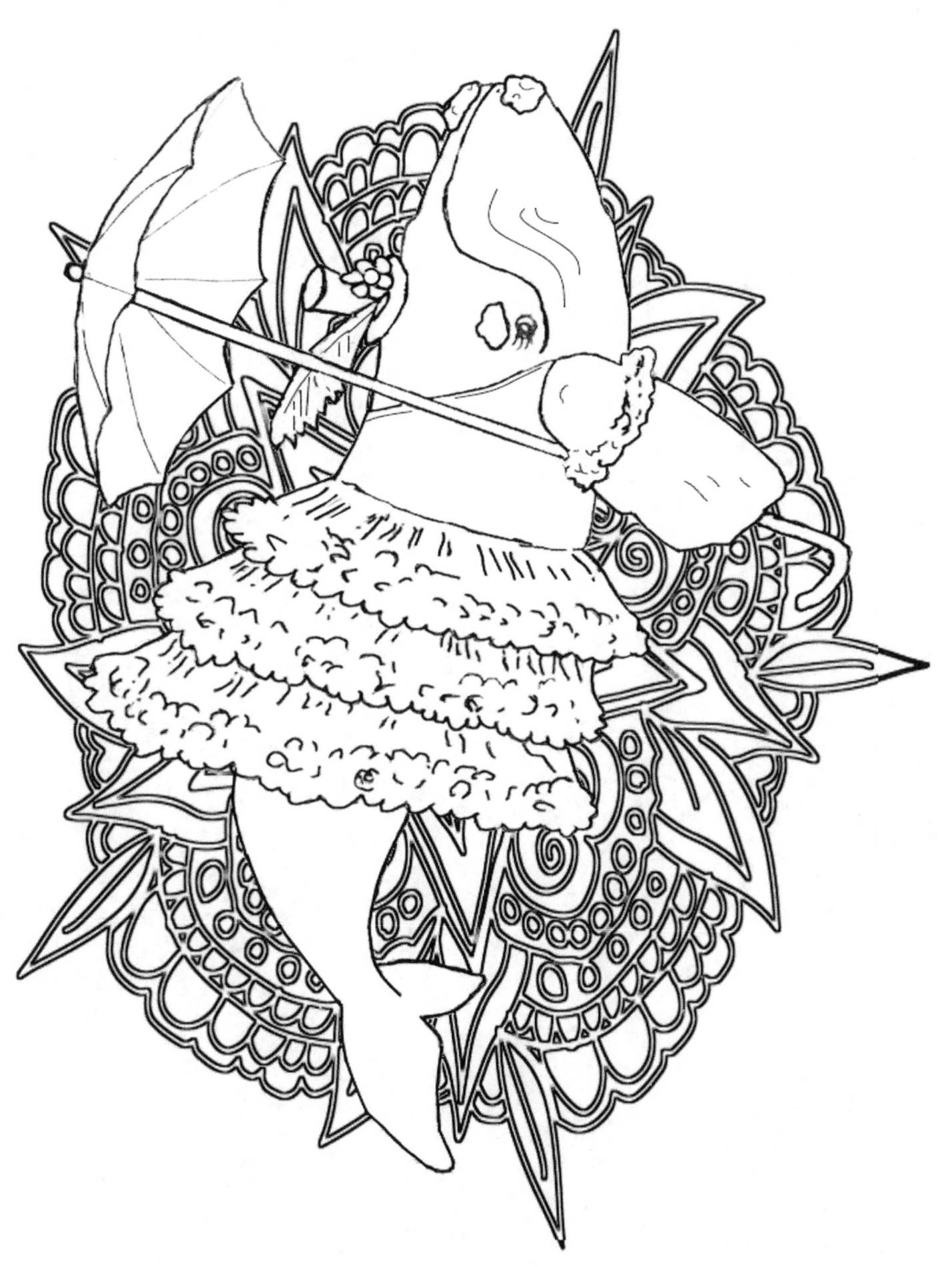

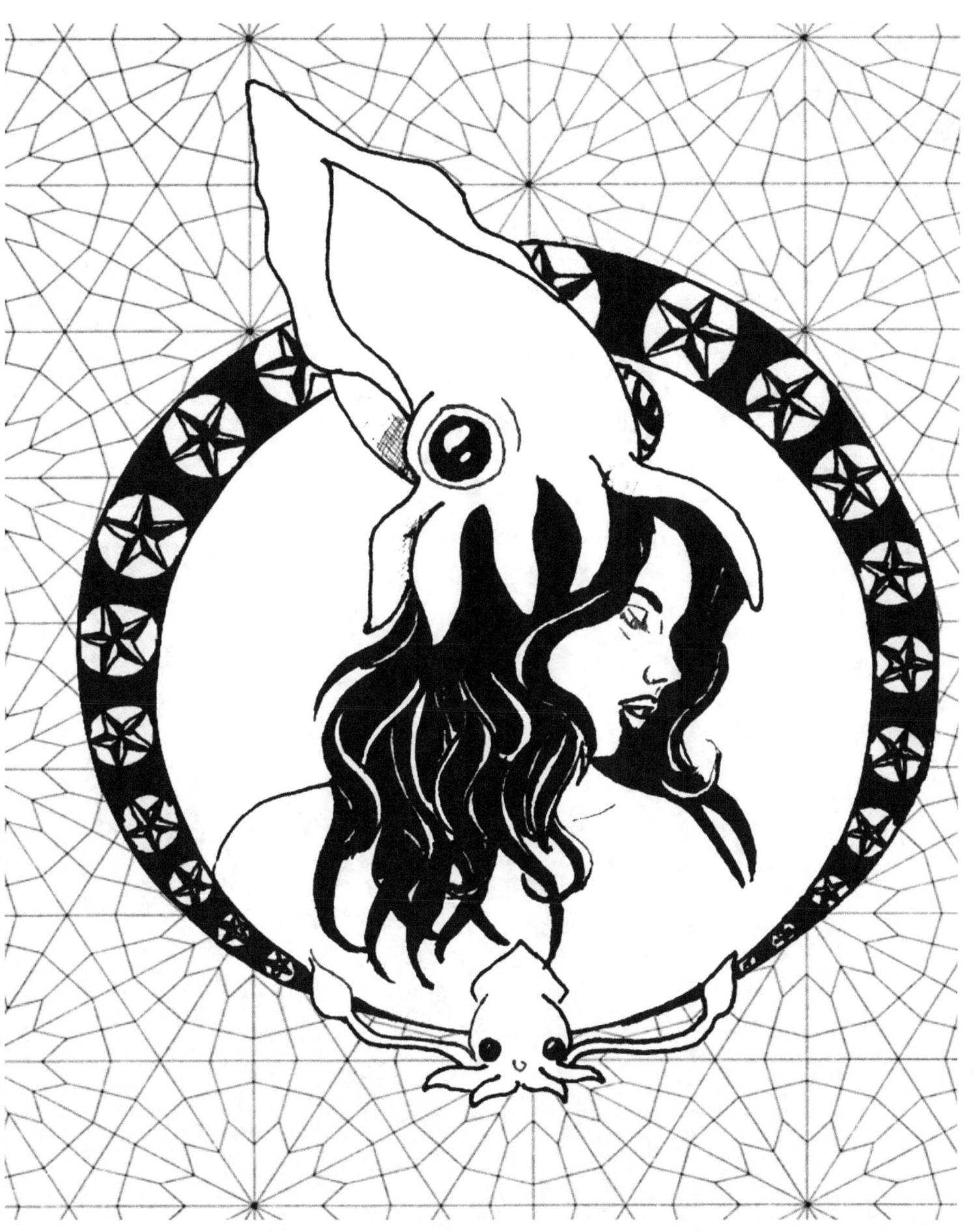

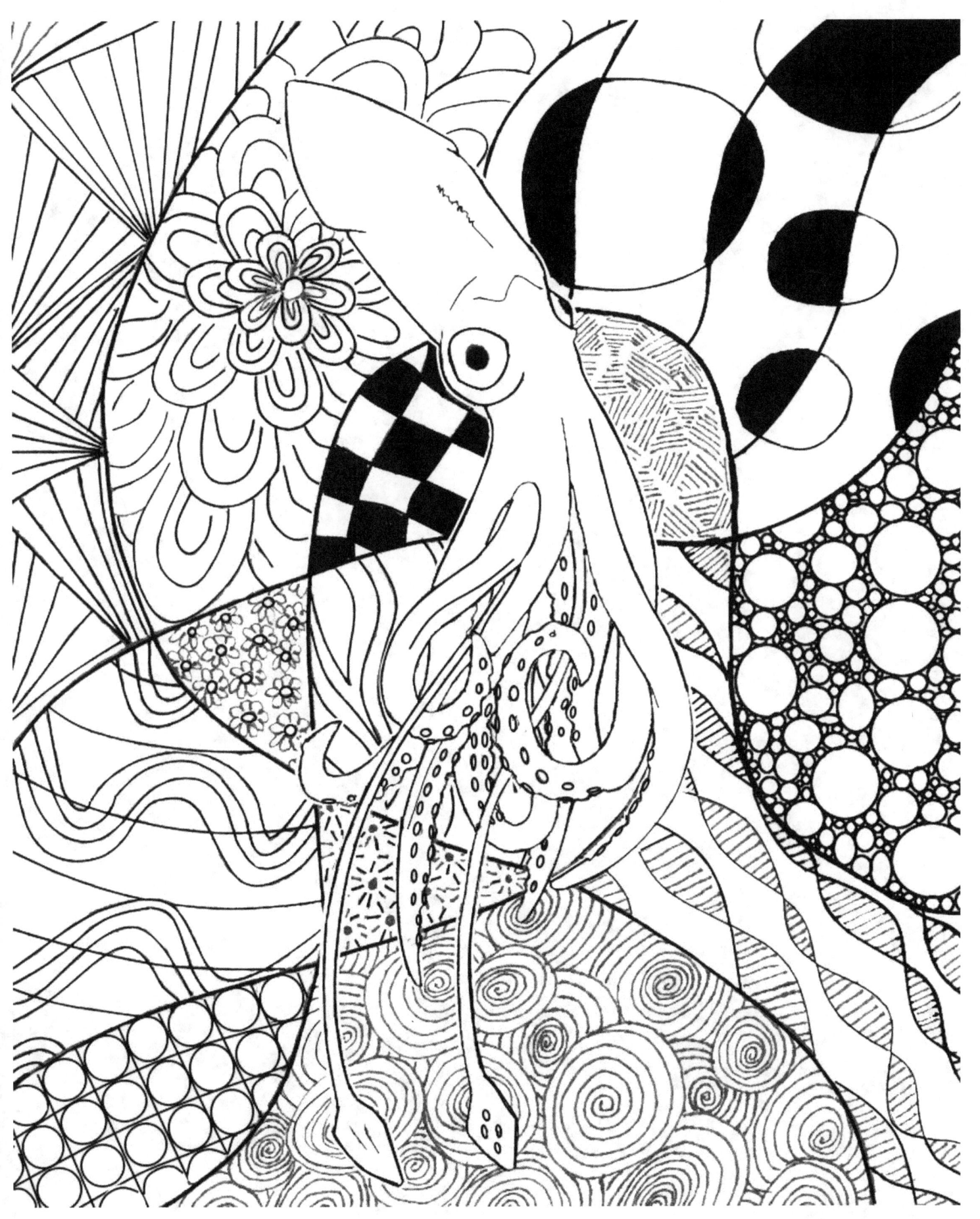

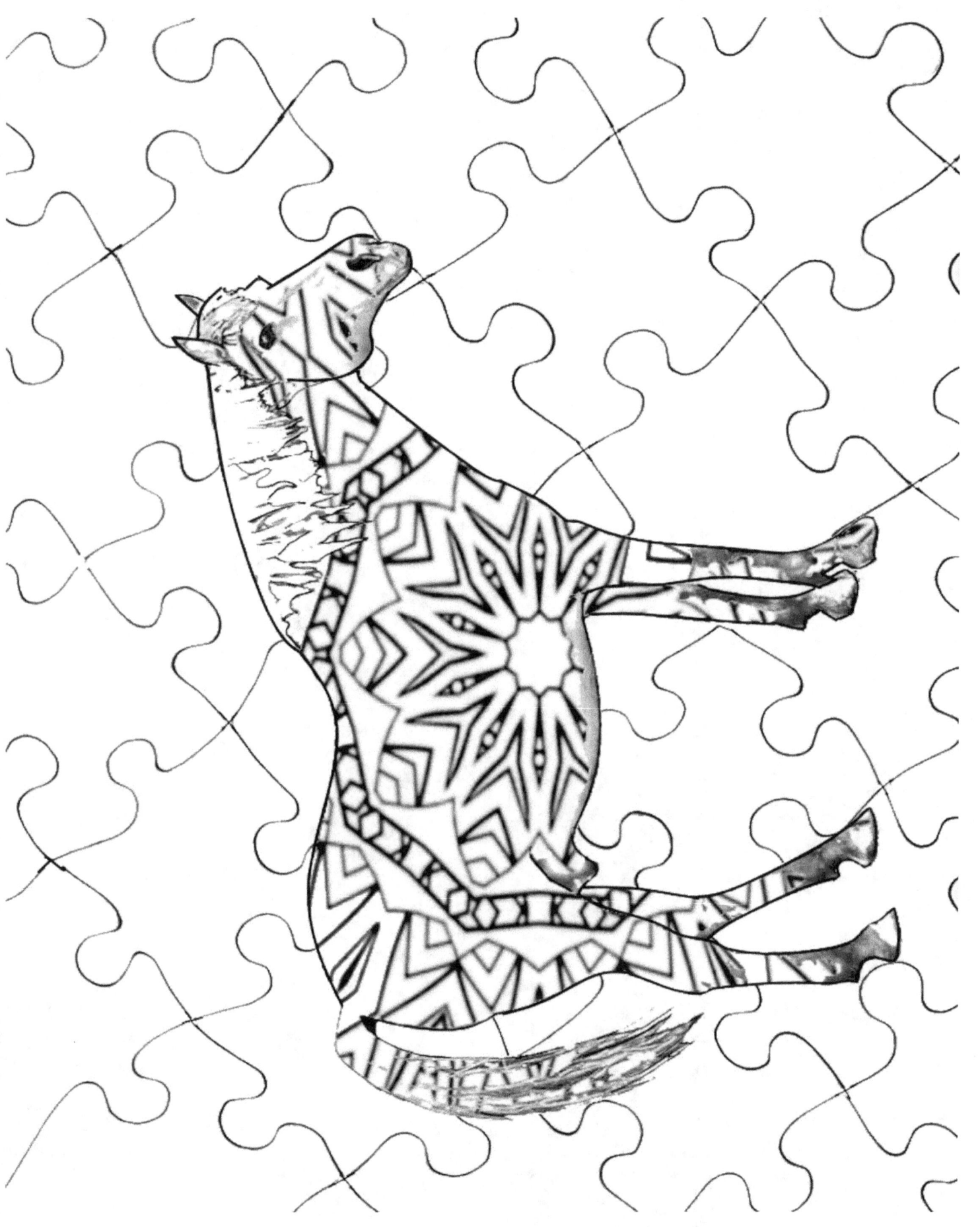

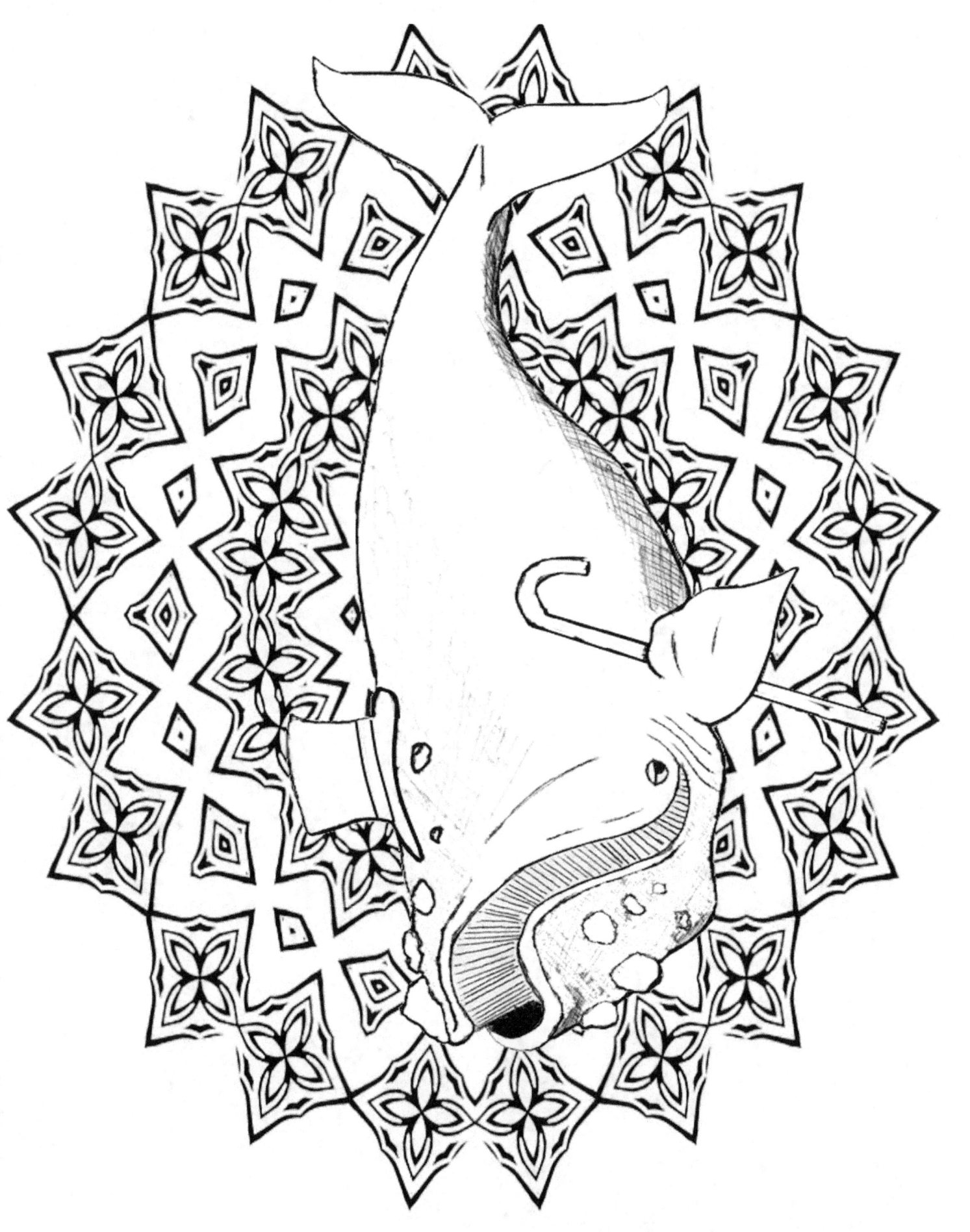

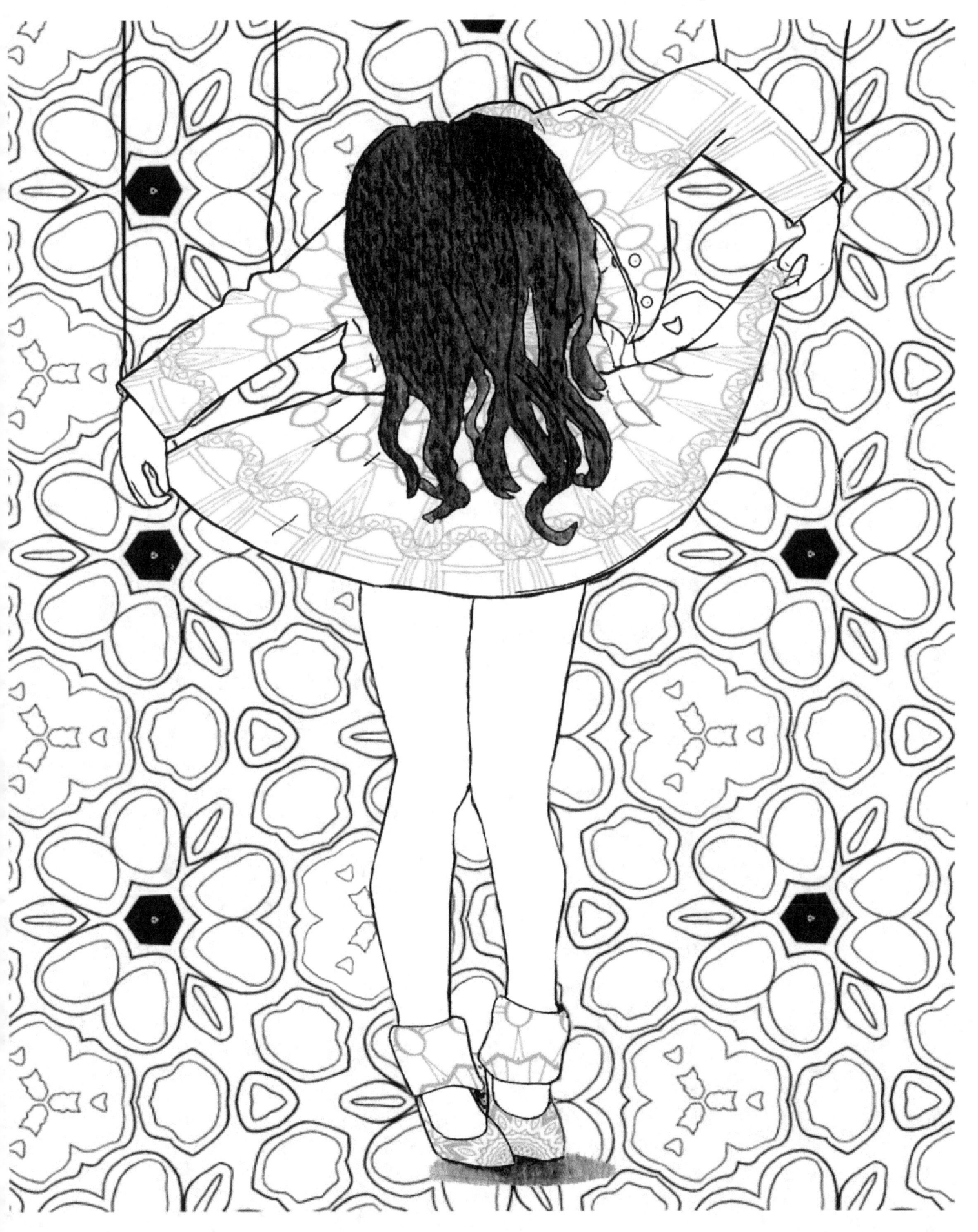

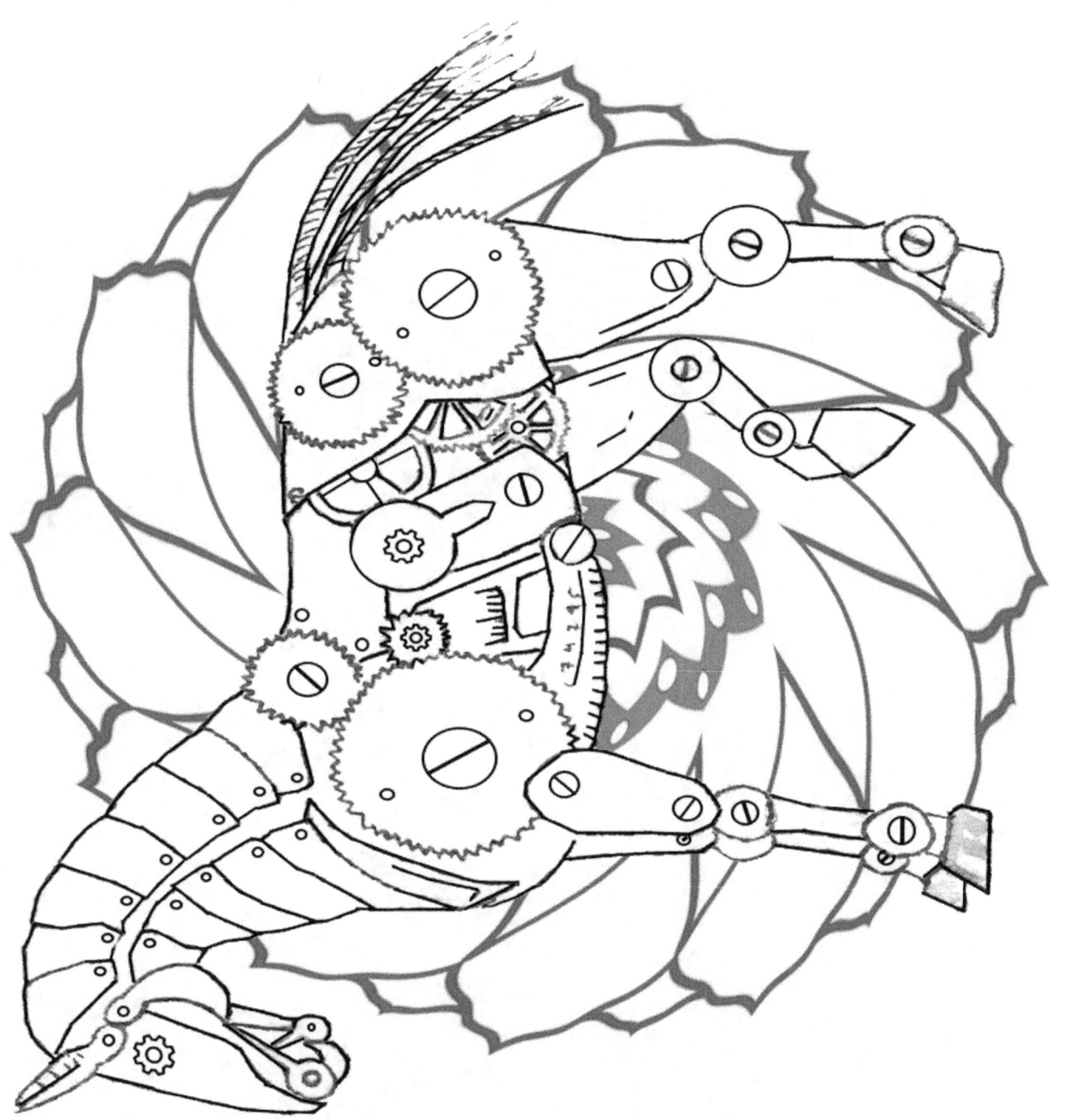

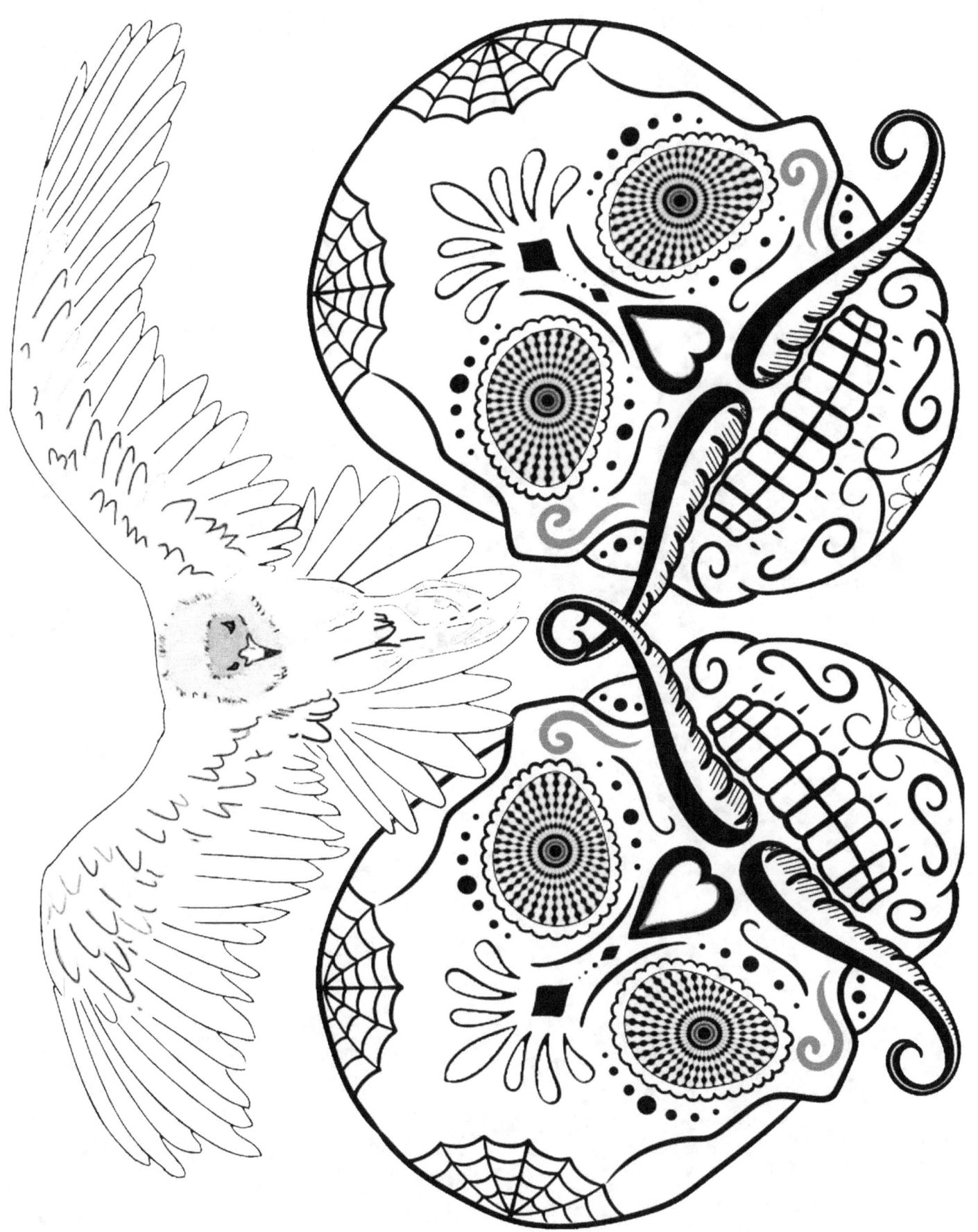

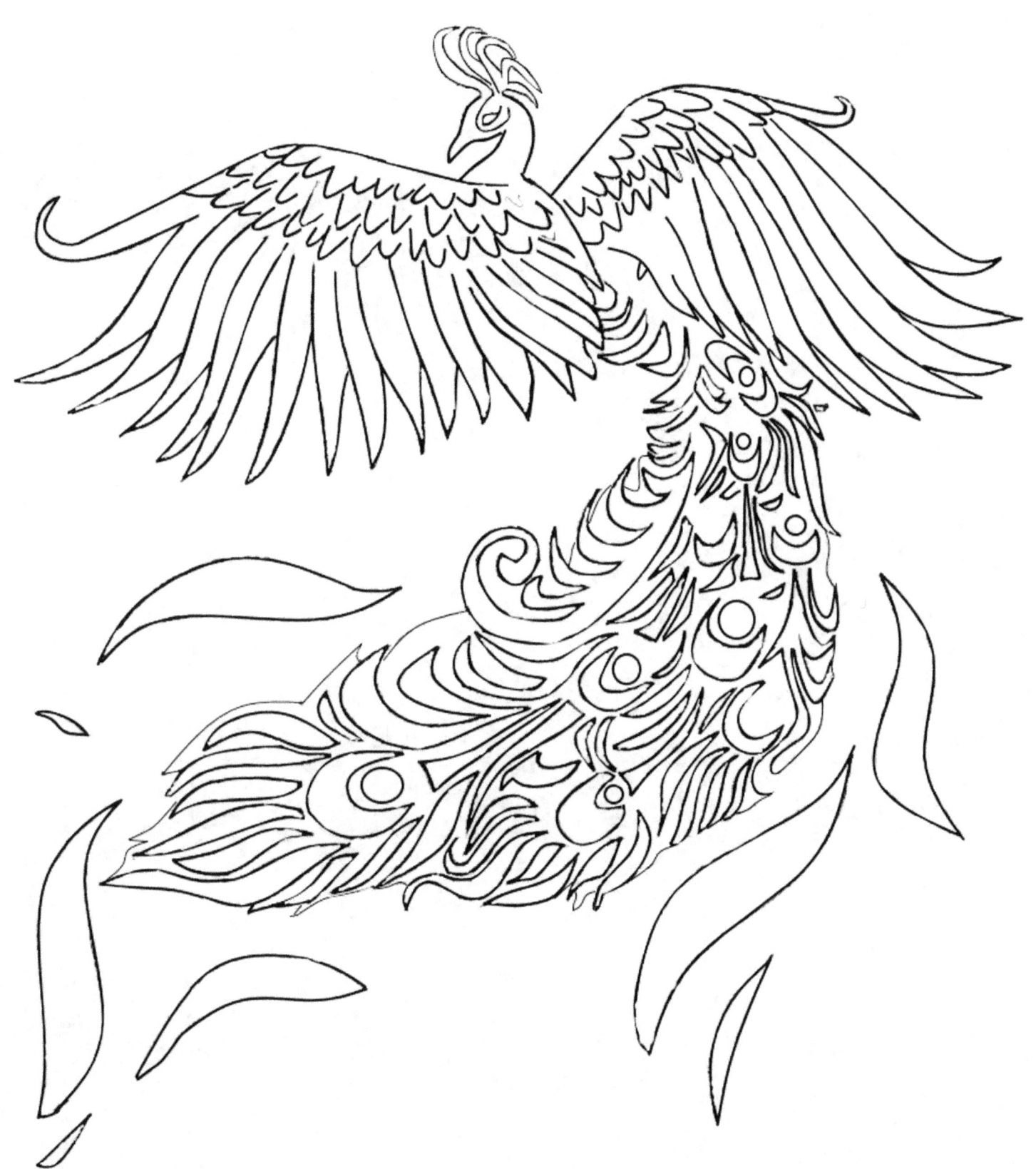

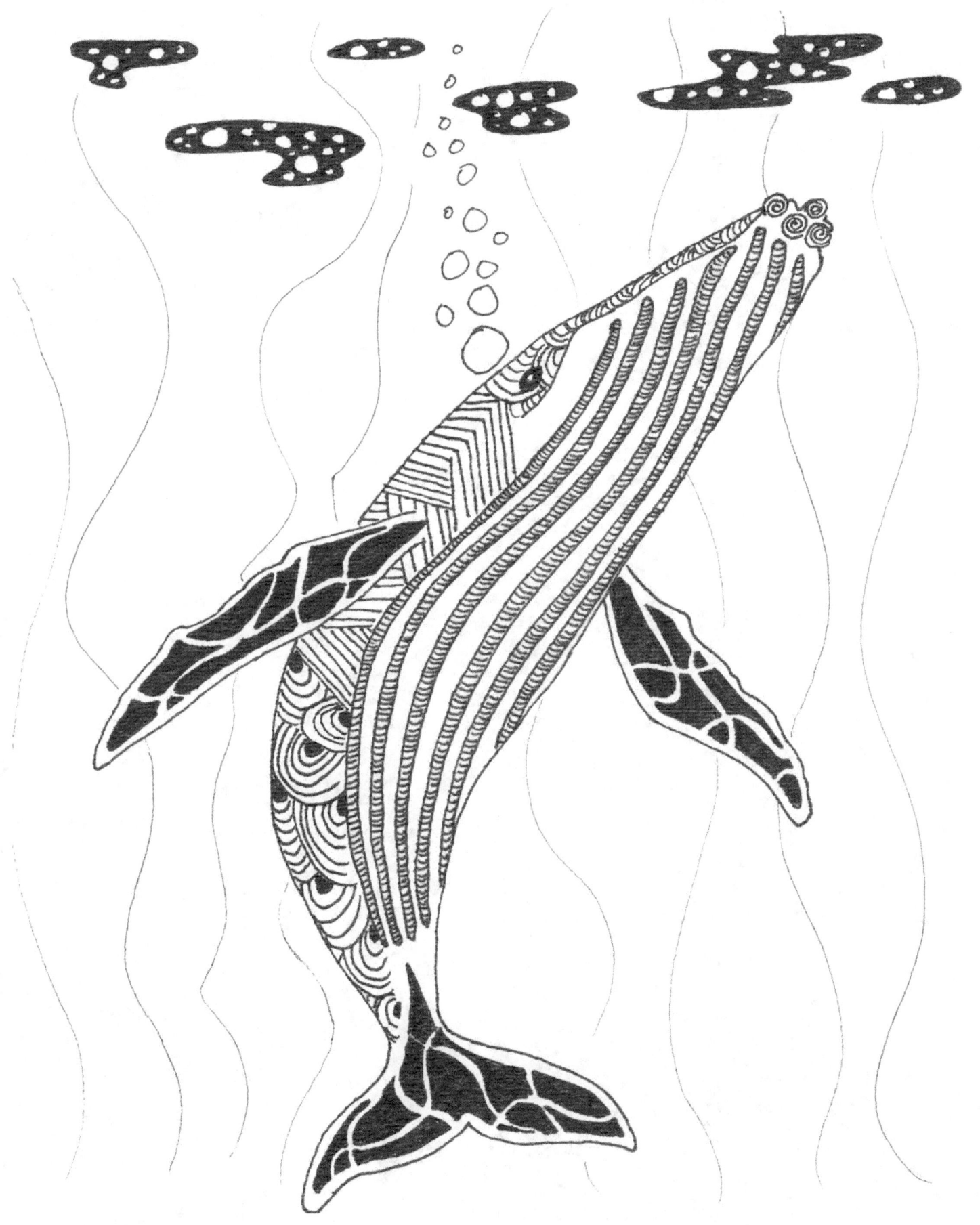

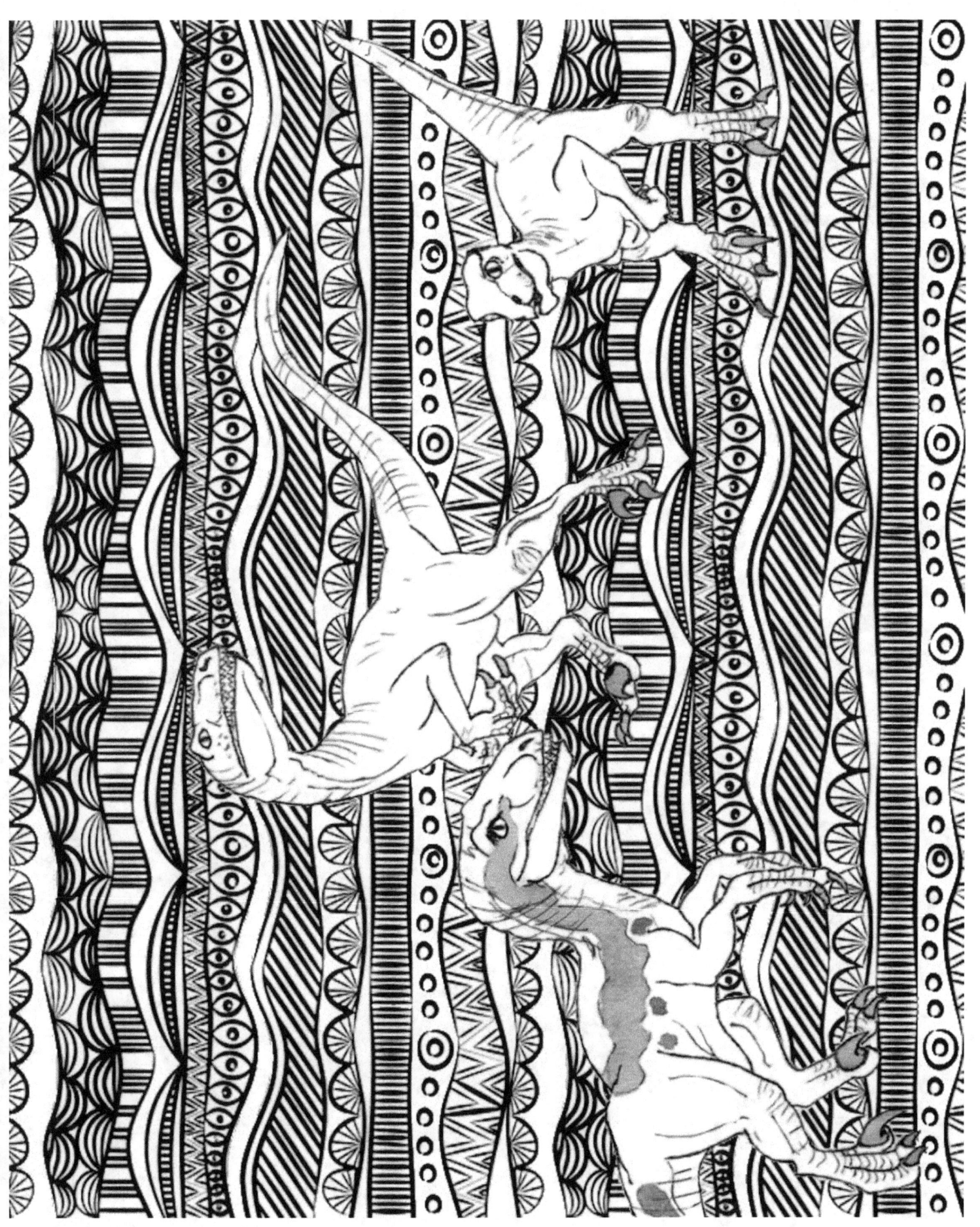

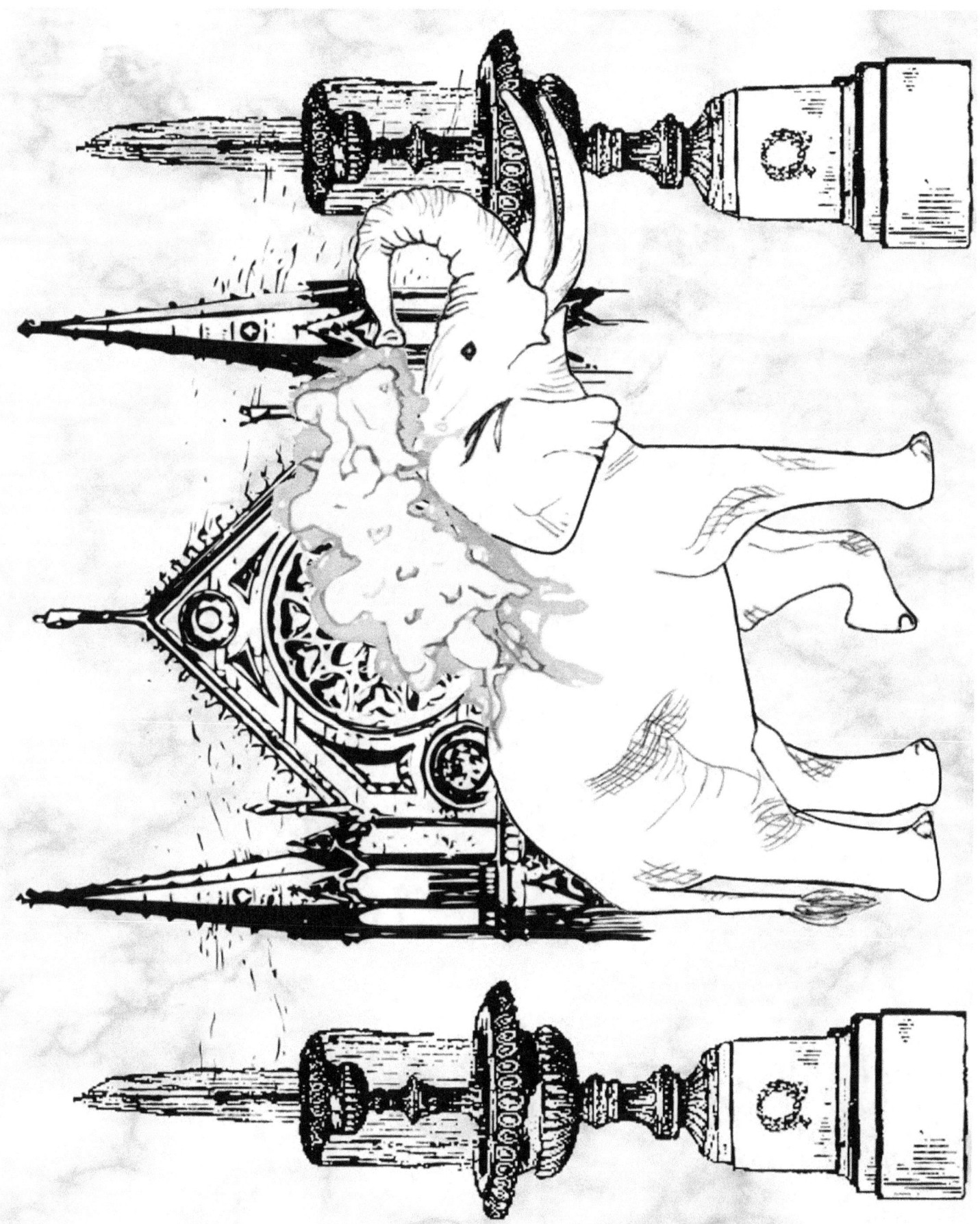

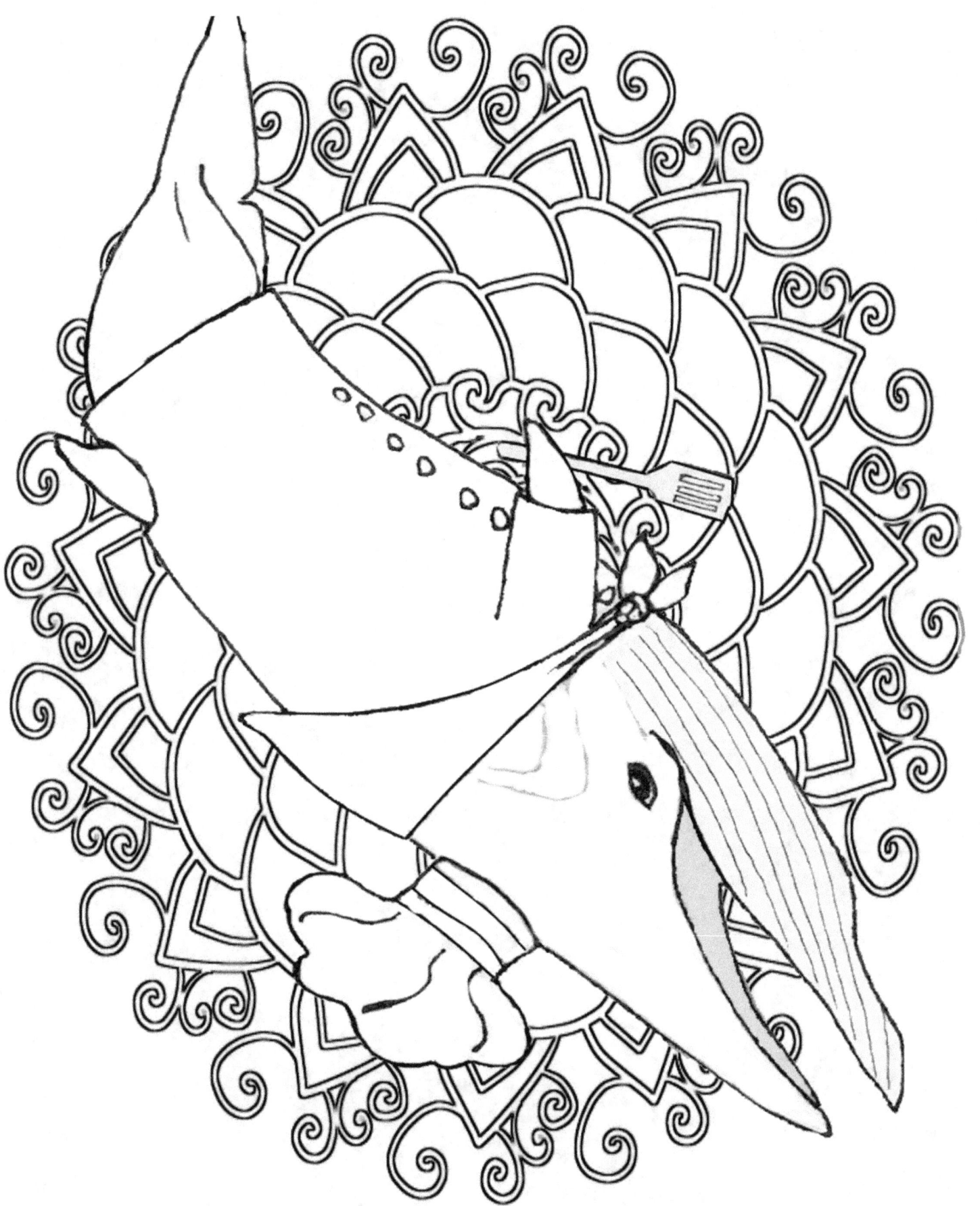

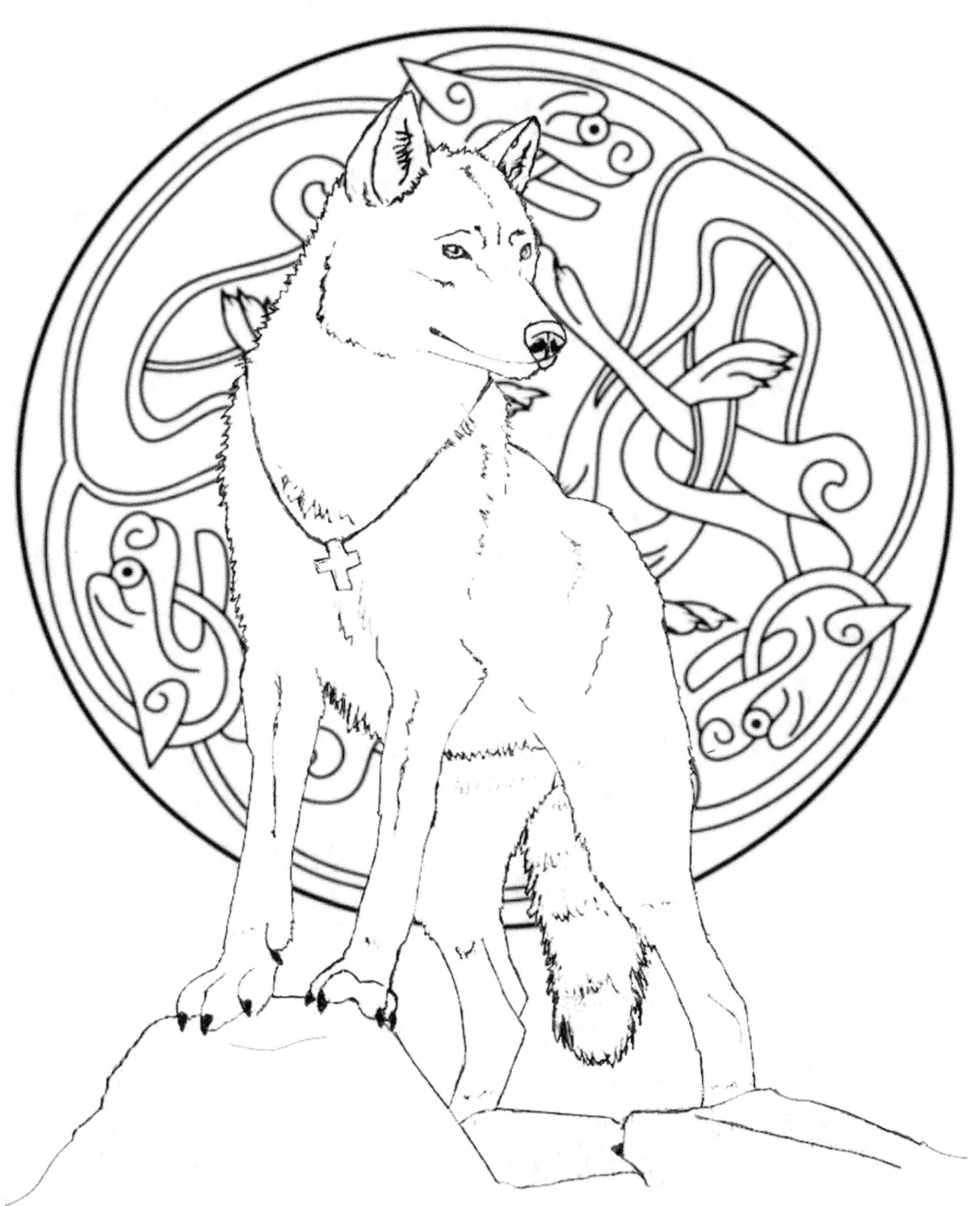

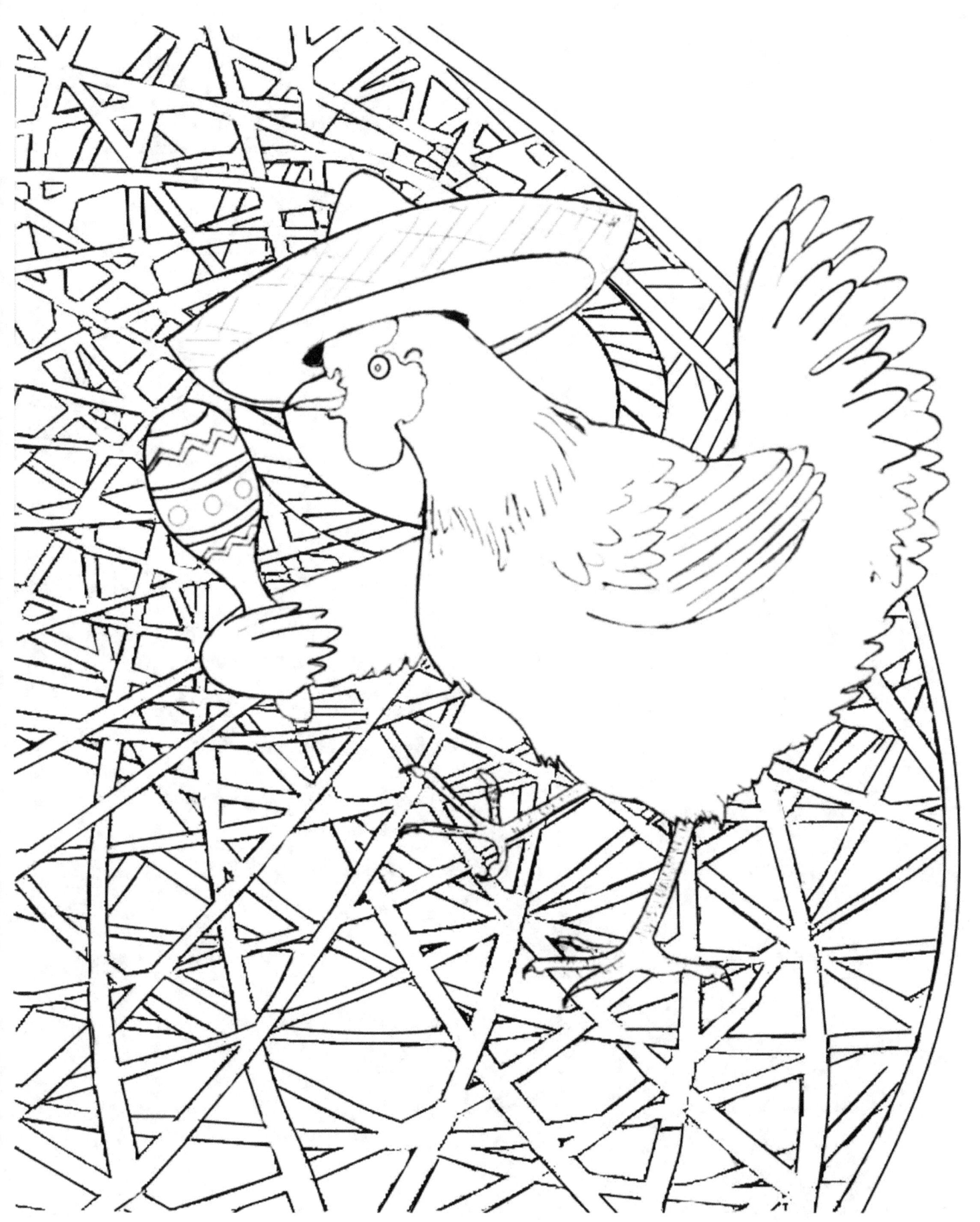

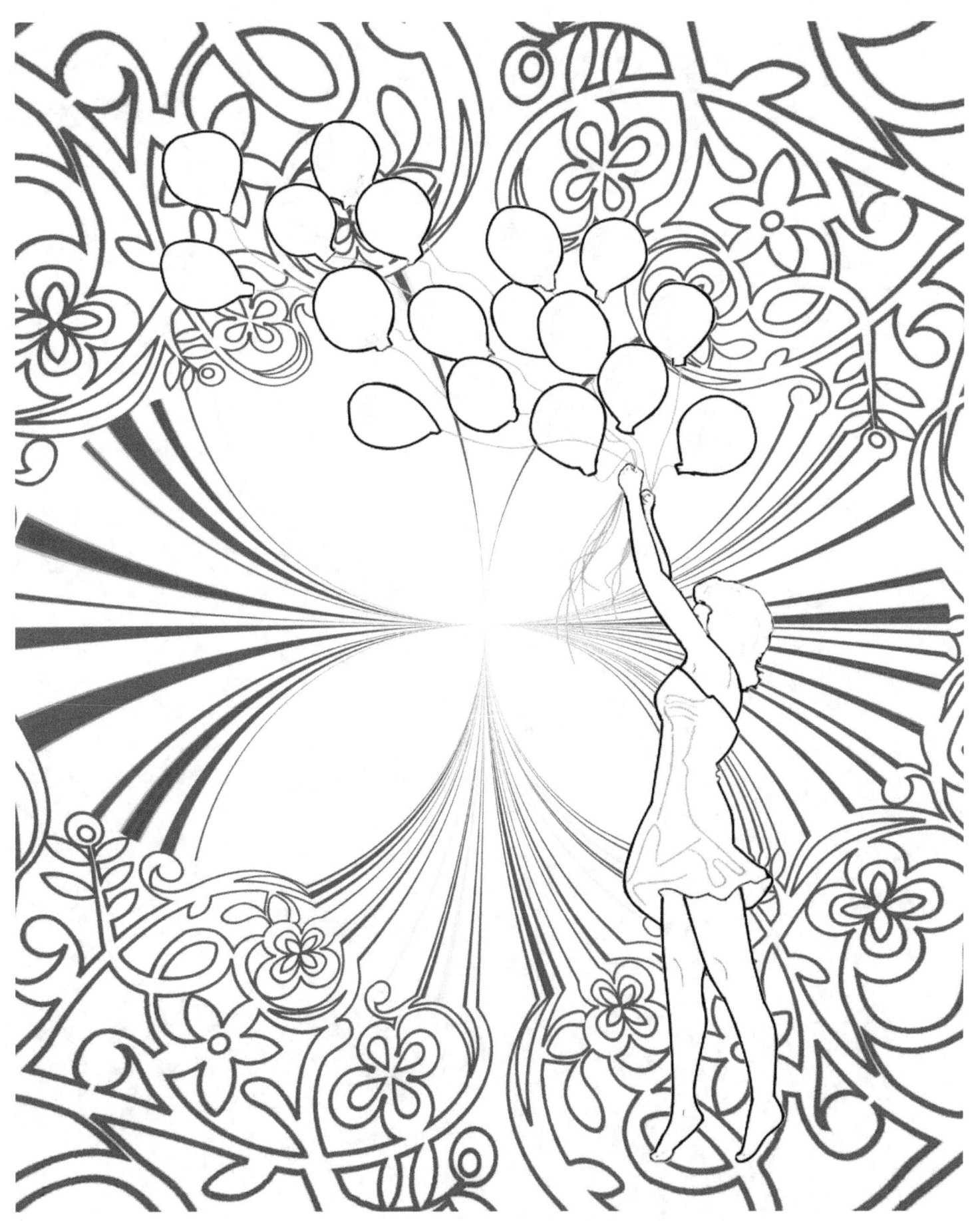

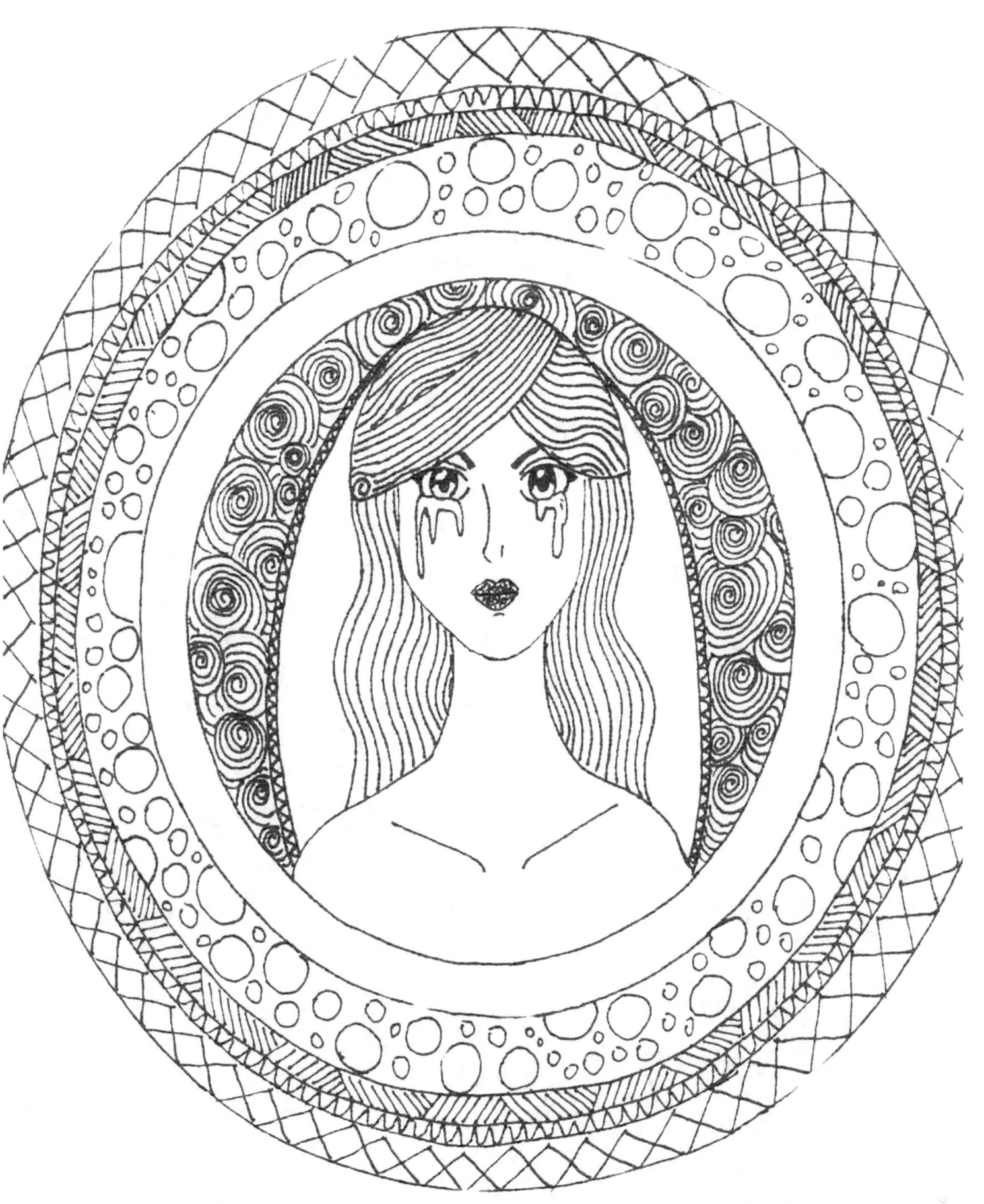

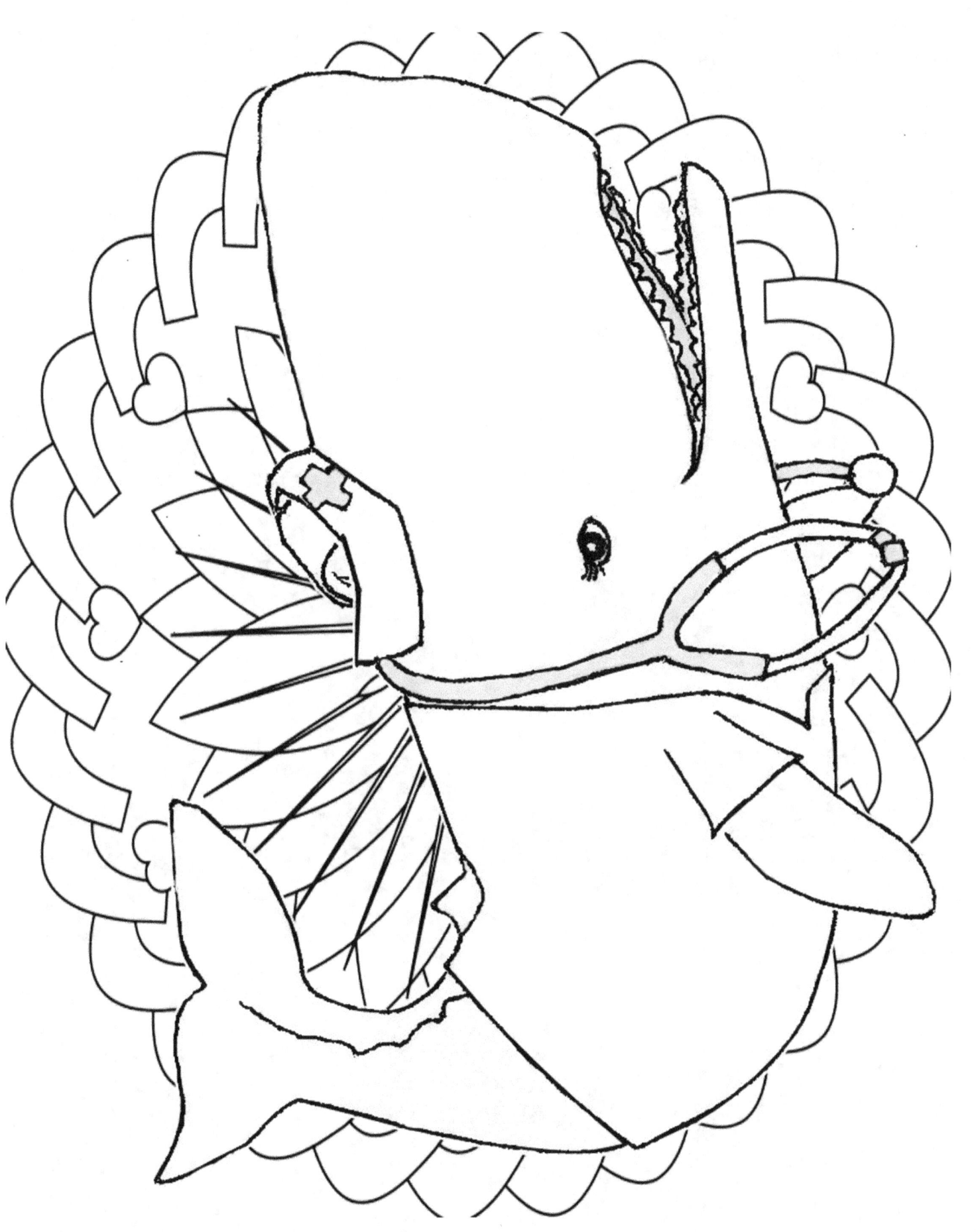

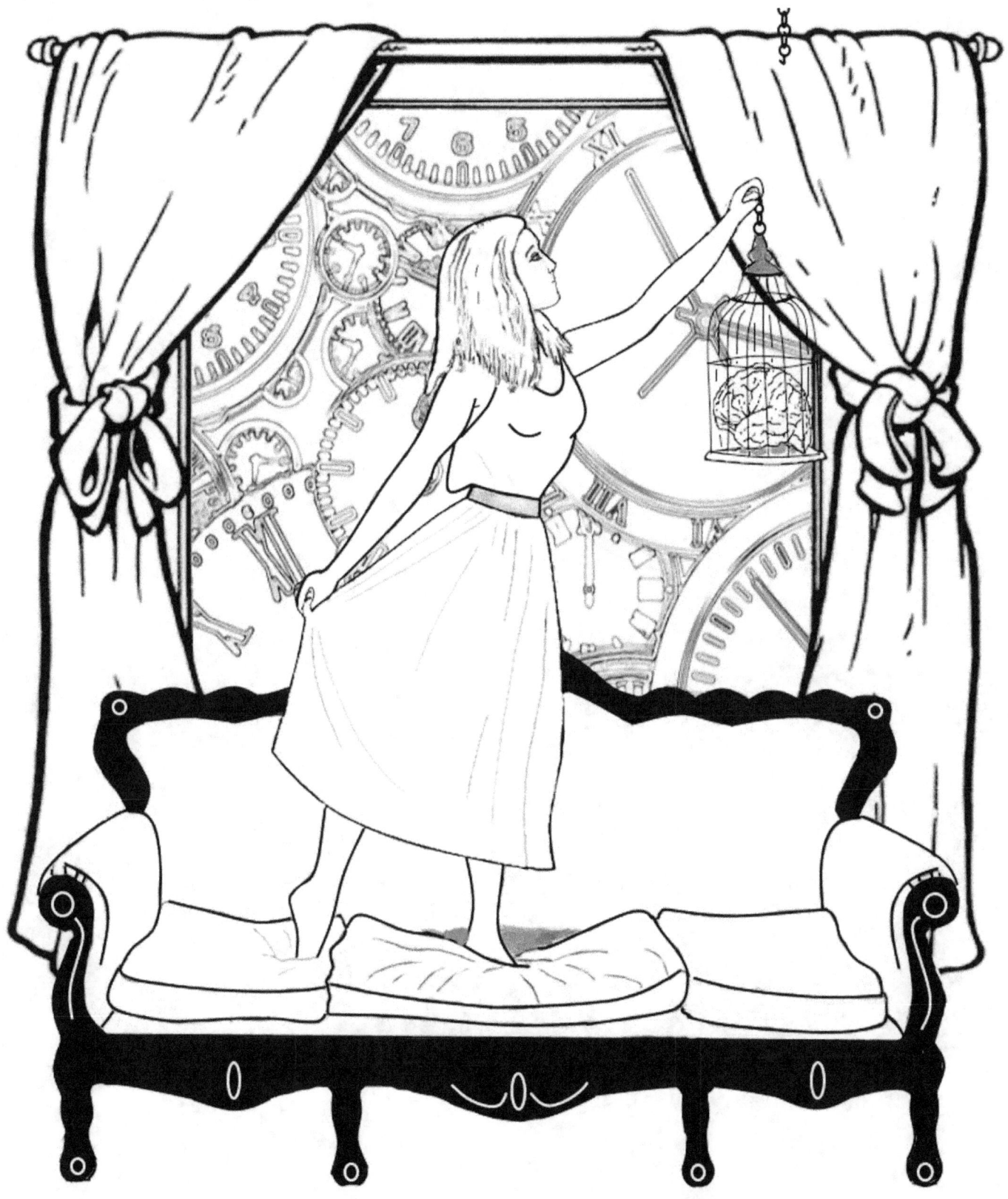

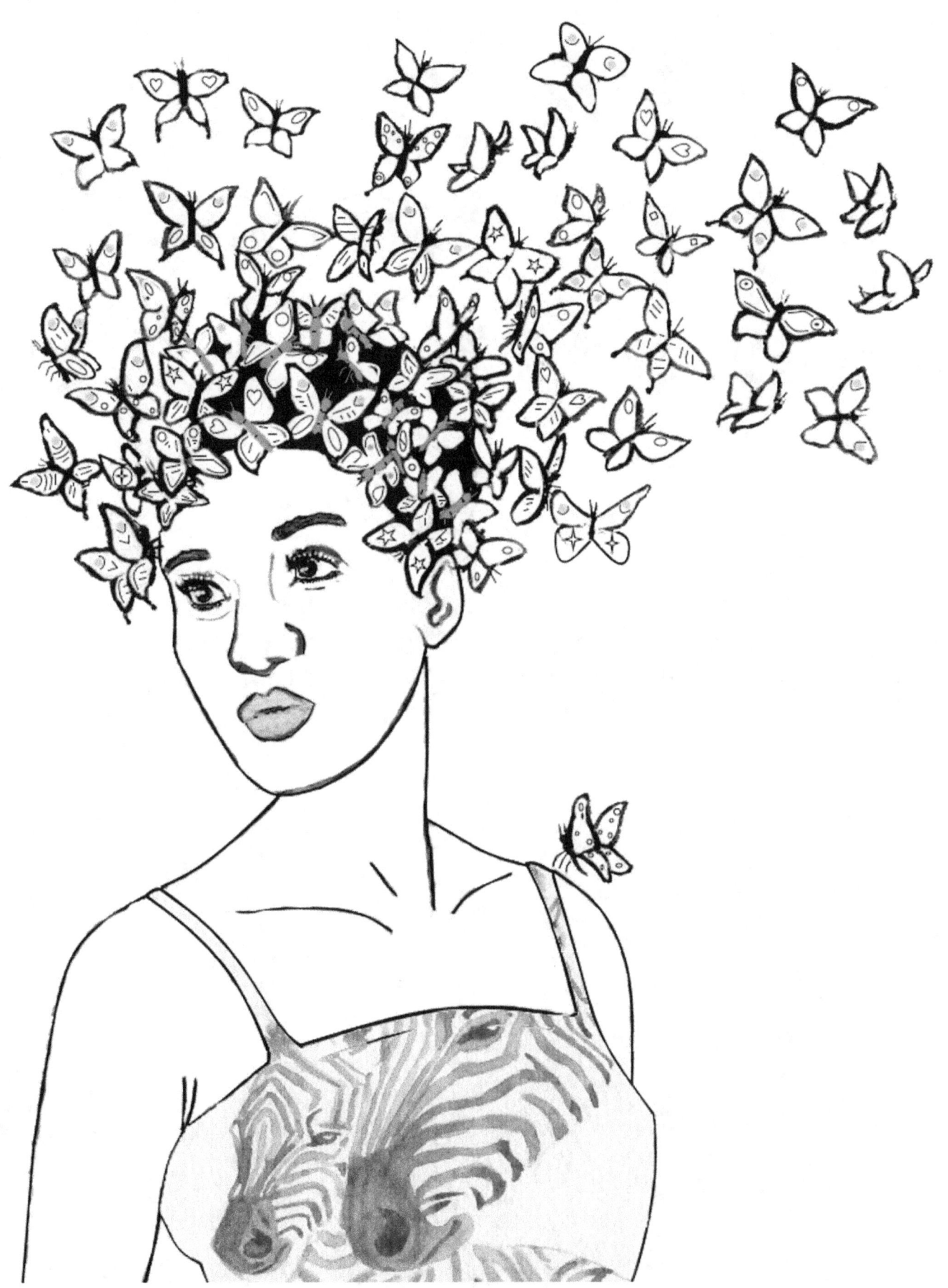

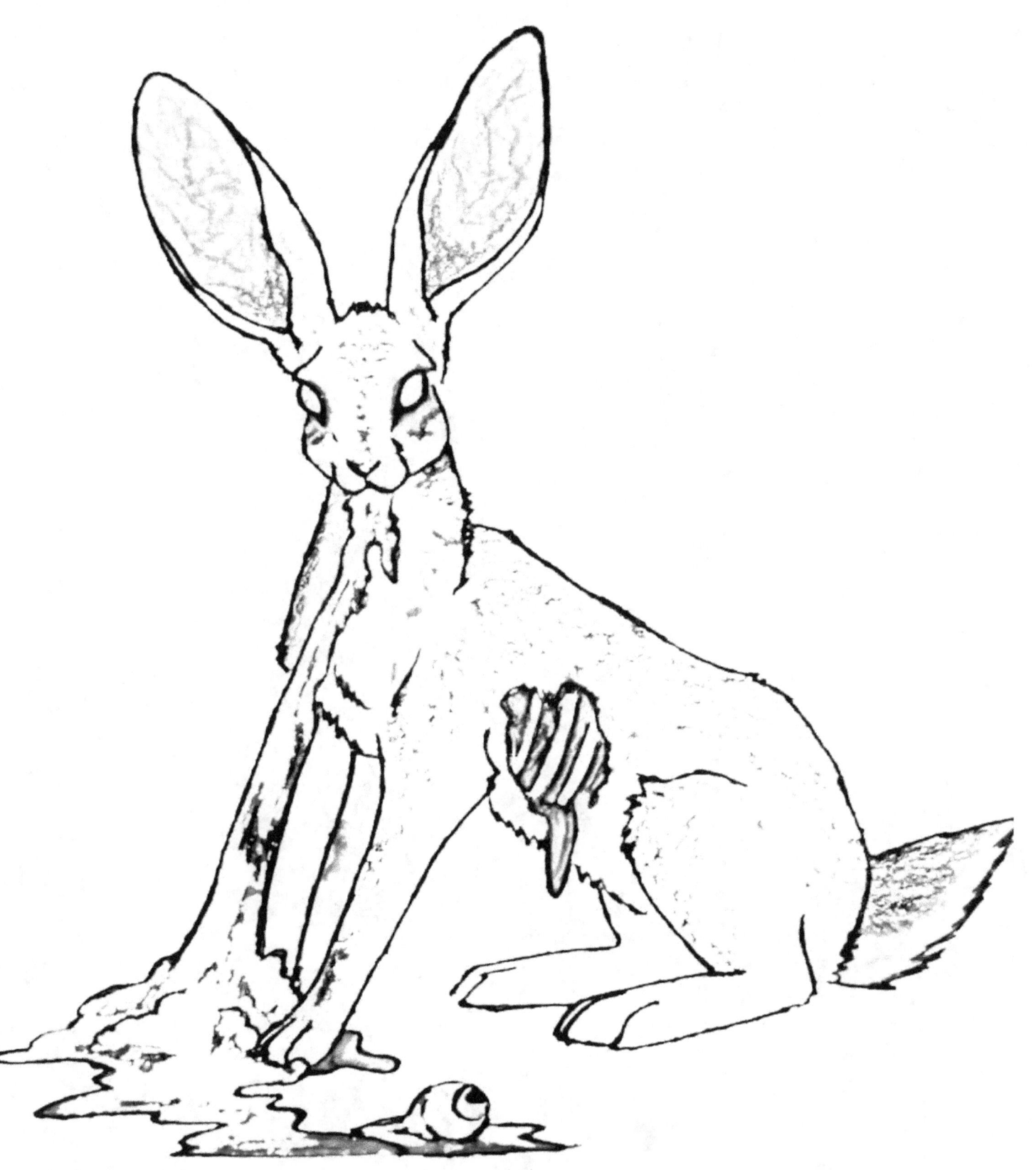

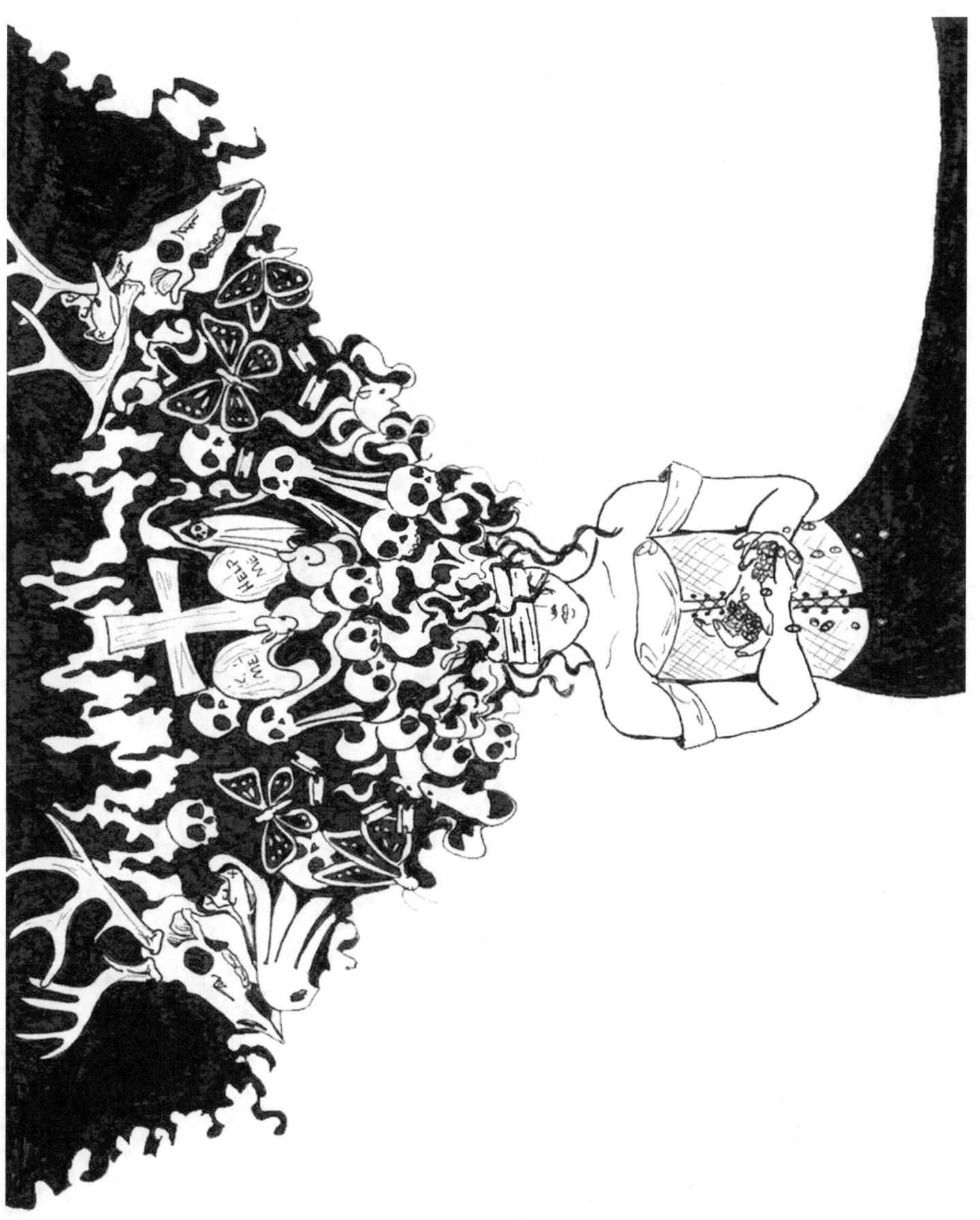

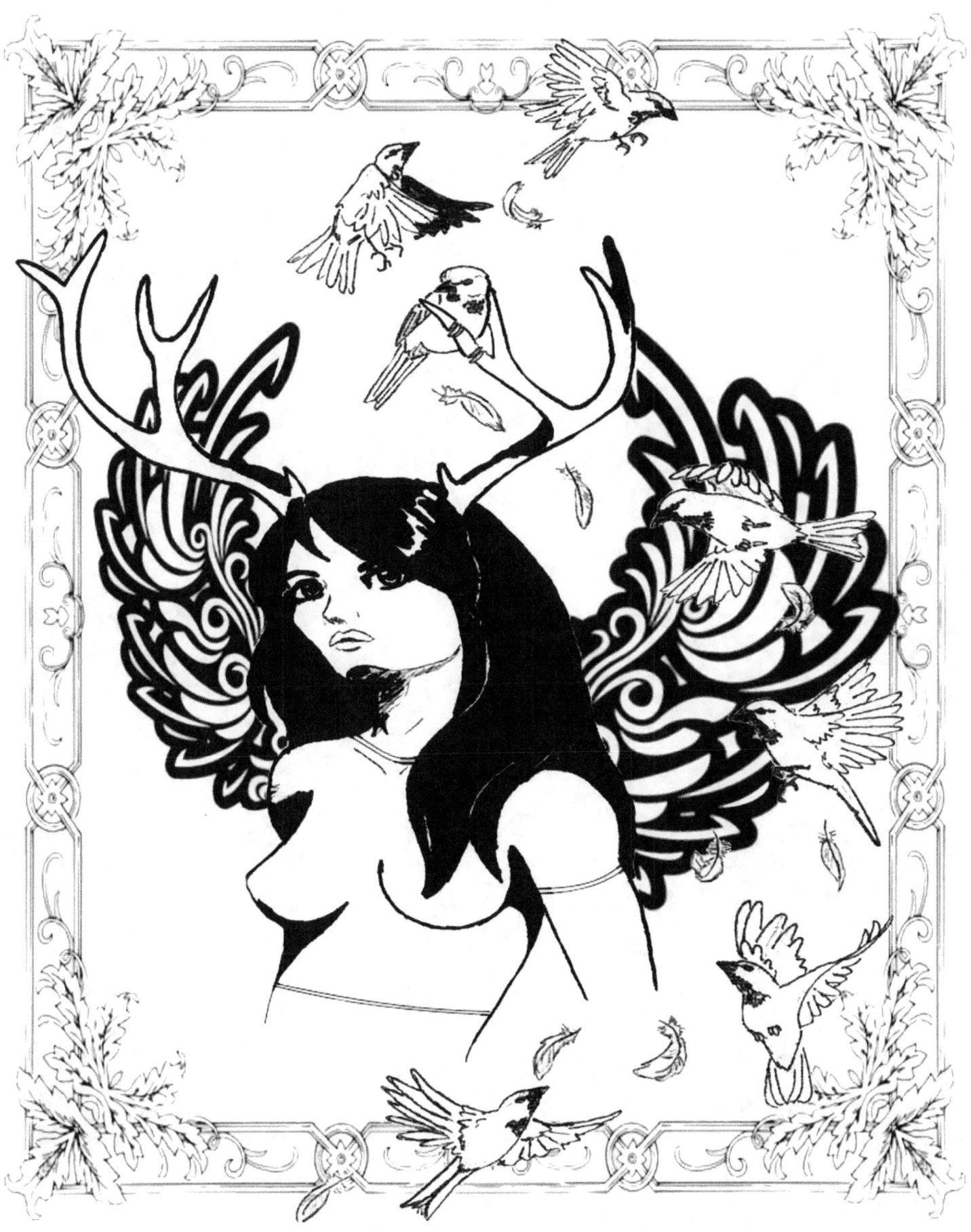

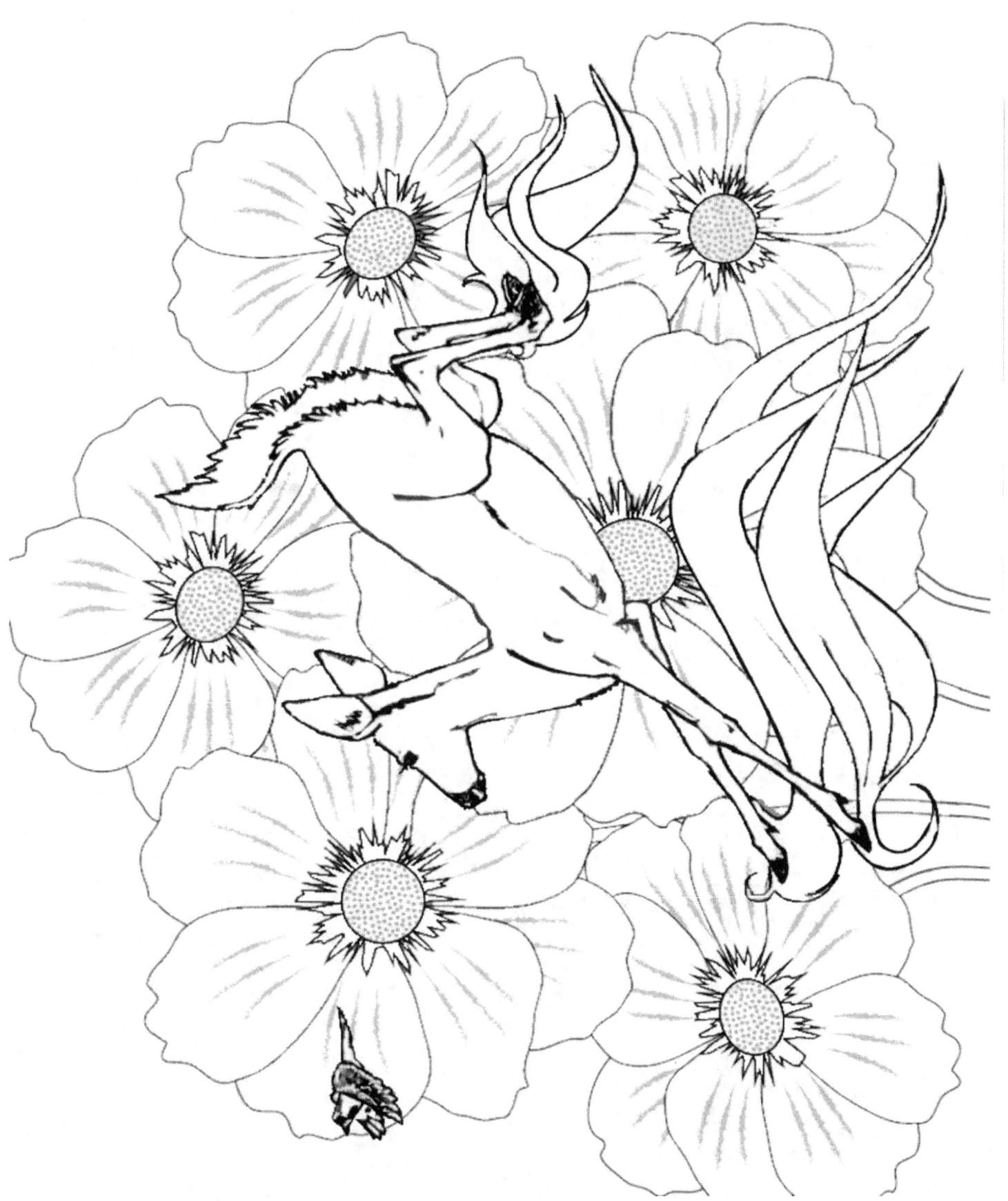

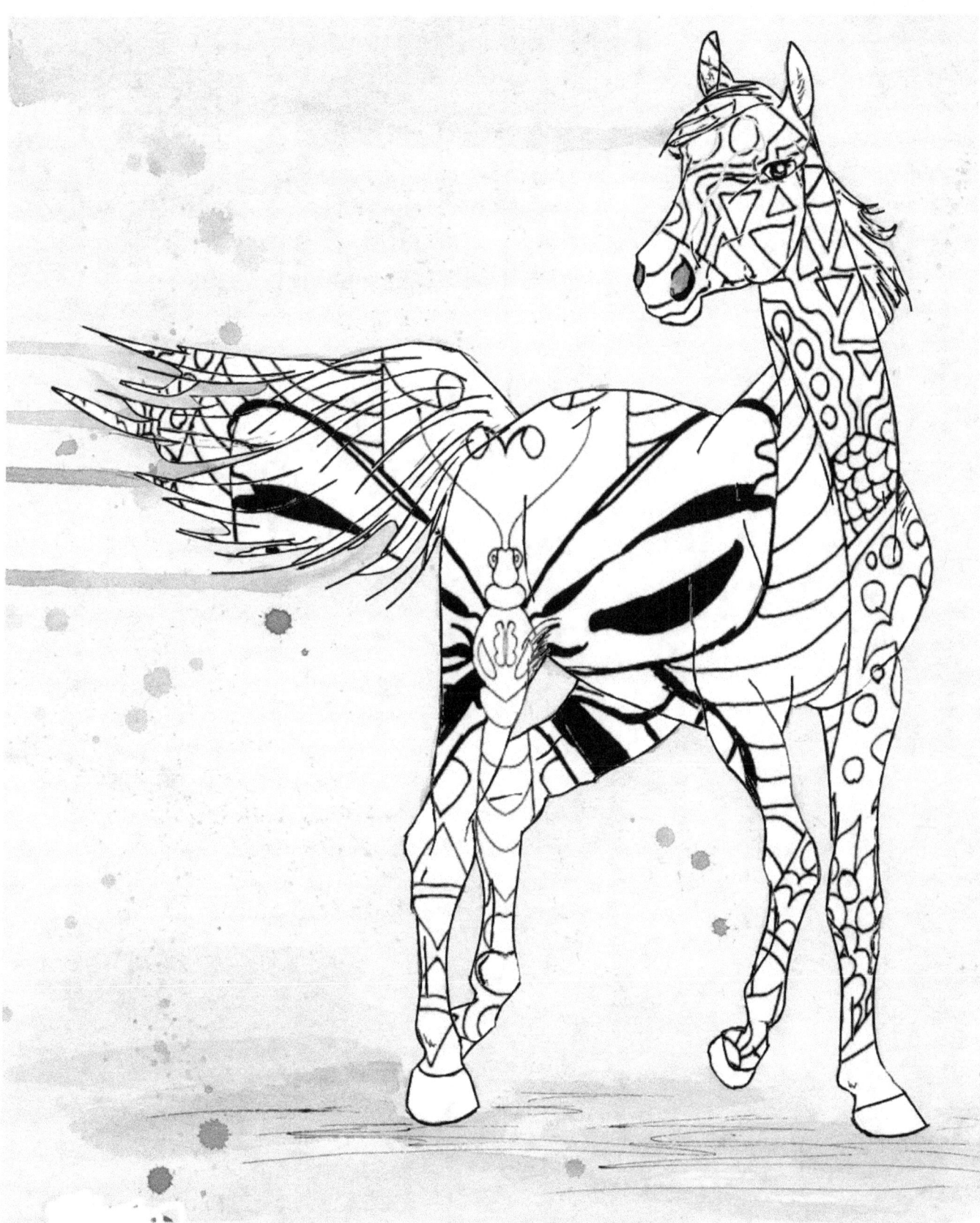

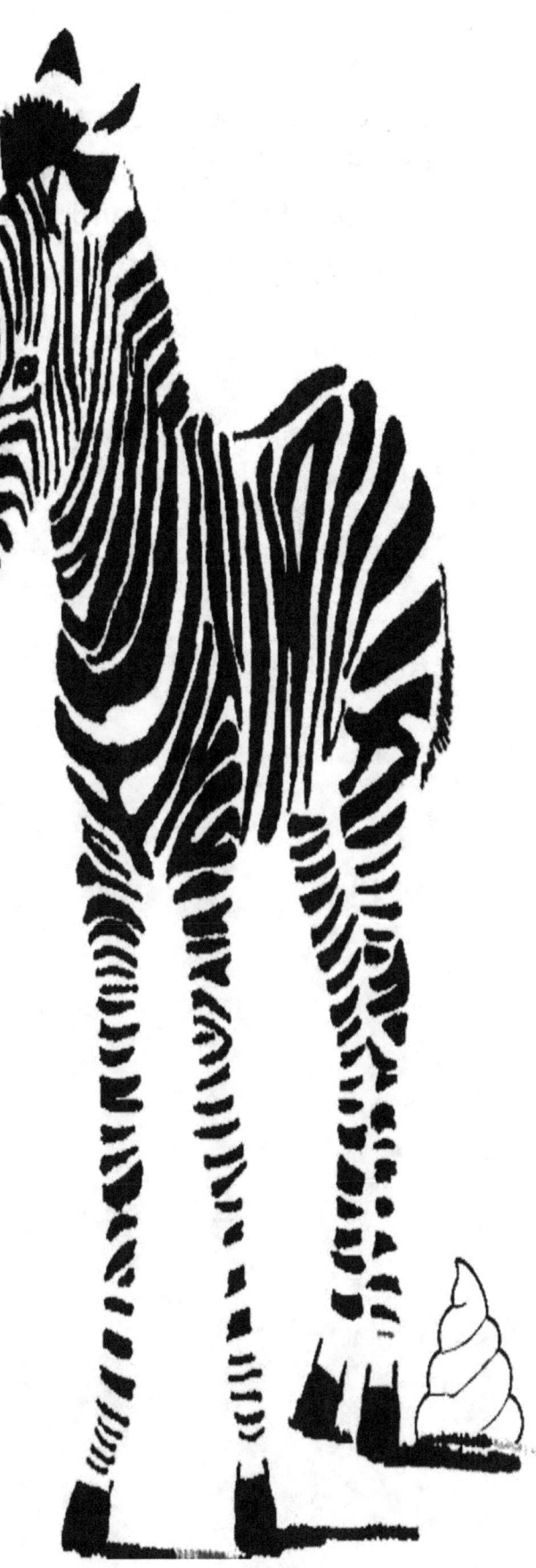

So...

I guess I'm done?

Special thanks to Jeremy Baird for editing and background art, Erica Casey for cover design, Kerstin Herrmann, Taoyuan, Emmie Norfolk, David Zydd, Kaylin Art, Gingertea, from the Pixabay community.

www.ingramcontent.com/pod-product-compliance
Lightning Source LLC
Chambersburg PA
CBHW081734220526
45468CB00008B/2092